Published by

The Naval & Military Press Ltd

Unit 5 Riverside, Brambleside
Bellbrook Industrial Estate
Uckfield, East Sussex
TN22 1QQ England

Tel: +44 (0)1825 749494

www.naval-military-press.com
www.nmarchive.com

HISTORY

OF THE

91st (SIEGE) BATTERY, R.G.A.

DECEMBER, 1915 to 11 NOVEMBER, 1918.

——————————

By MAJOR W. F. CHRISTIAN, D.S.O., R.G.A.

The Naval & Military Press Ltd

CONTENTS.

INTRODUCTION.

THE following notes have been written for ex-members of the Battery as a record of our comradeship in arms.

They are little more than a rough diary of events with a few remarks interspersed. The lists of targets engaged will make tedious reading, but I have included them to make the record of our work complete as far as possible.

I hope that the mention of the various places we visited will revive old scenes and bring back some memories without regrets.

I have included in the appendix a list of all the addresses which I have been able to collect of old members of the Battery. Officers can always be addressed as c/o Cox & Co., 16, Charing Cross, London, S.W.

I have let myself go, so to speak, here and there when writing of the Battery and its achievements; but I am tremendously proud of having commanded 91st Siege Battery, I have never met a better one. I want to express again my deepest gratitude to all you officers, N.C.O's and men who served me with such blind loyalty.

I greatly regret the fact that gradually failing health towards the end of the War prevented me from giving my best efforts, especially during those last glorious three months.

Good luck to you all.

Tynemouth.

January, 1920.

CHAPTER I.

BIRTH AND EARLY DAYS.

On December 1st, 1915, I joined at Plymouth with the temp. rank of Major, and orders to form 91st Siege Battery. Officers were to be posted by W.O., the N.C.O's to be regulars posted from Bexhill, and the men to be posted from R.G.A. Plymouth. During the first week the following joined : Capt. Leslie Smith, and Lieut. C. H. Scholefield, Lieut. W. B. Neilson, 2nd Lieut. B. C. Thompson, and 2nd Lieut. R. Shrive.* I was allowed to do a little picking and choosing to get suitable men, and anxious work it was finding enough talent to supply the large number of necessary specialists. Finally a good team of Kitchener men was decided upon and so the Battery was born. They were all volunteers of course, and eagerly embraced the opportunity of "having a dip at the Huns". Some men applied for their brothers or chums to be allowed to join and this was arranged where possible. There was no war weariness those days and everyone entered into the game with heart and soul. Very soon the spirit of 91 became evident, we all felt it, though seldom spoke of it, and it carried us right through to the sweet end. It is remarkable that a newly formed unit without traditions, could develope spontaneously such a fine *esprit*; it was very real and very compelling, fostered by mutual trust, and a feeling that we were capable of doing big things. Every Officer, N.C.O. and man was proud to belong to the Battery, it will always be our proudest boast—we were smart on parade, smart when we walked out, good at games and tried hard to learn our job and do it.

When getting the Battery together at Plymouth I managed incidentally to get together a very fine football team and we and their many opponents thought a lot about them. At Plymouth and Horsham after many games against military teams we held an unbeaten record and I told B.S.M. Newton to look out for an unbeaten military team of that season. Next day he told me that the Irish Guards had not been beaten ; it looked like infernal cheek for a little unit 150 strong to challenge the Irish Guards who had many hundreds to pick from—still, we did it, and a match was arranged at Horsham one Saturday afternoon in February 1916. The Guards team was very gallant and sportsmanlike and a splendid game resulted to our surprise in a victory for us of 2—0. Our opponents were most anxious for a return match and one was arranged to take place on their ground a fortnight later. It took place before a large crowd and resulted in our winning again by 4—0. We began to get ourselves talked about and I don't think it did us any harm. We played many other matches including three tremendous games with 102 Siege Battery at Lydd, each of which ended in a draw, and when we went to France in May 1916 the team was still unbeaten. I dwell somewhat on the football team because it did much to foster the spirit of 91.

---

* 2nd Lieut. Shrive and myself were still with the battery at the end of the war.

Let it not be imagined that our chief energies were devoted to football. From the beginning those of us who knew anything about our job devoted ourselves to instructing others. Classes were formed for Signallers, B.C.A's Observers and Layers and all went smoothly, for all wanted to learn. After about one month at Plymouth we moved to Horsham where we had the assistance of a School of Gunnery and the use of guns, directors, dial sights, and signalling equipment.

Shortly after our arrival at Horsham Capt. Leslie Smith was replaced by Capt. H. A. Cox and he was in turn replaced by Temp. Capt. R. H. A. Kellie who had served with me in 34 Siege Battery under Major H. R. Brancker in 1915. 34 S.B. was composed originally of regulars and had done a lot of splendid pioneer work with 9·2″ Howitzers.

About the middle of April we moved to Lydd and having done some more intensive training and six shoots from 6″ and obsolete 8″ Howitzers we were deemed ready to take our part in the great adventure.

We were very pleased on hearing that we were to be equipped with 9·2″ Howitzers, I especially, because I thought I knew all about them. The resulting confidence may have been useful but it led to disillusionment too often in the days that were to come.

On May 5th the Battery proceeded to Bristol to mobilize. Capt. Kellie and 29 other ranks went to Woolwich to draw guns and stores.

From May 7th onwards guns and stores arrived daily. The guns were mounted and gun drill was carried out.

The ladies of Bristol looked with favouring eye upon the budding warriors and did much to make our stay there a pleasant one. Some tender episodes must have taken place there to judge from the large number of letters addressed to Bristol which the Officers had to censor in France. I have heard it said that other Batteries which mobilized there received similar marks of favour—I give this statement for what it is worth.

Concerning the censoring of letters—I hope that in future wars when this has to be done that Officers outside the units—say at brigade headquarters—will be detailed for the duty. It is most unpleasant to have to read of the private affairs of men with whom you are in daily contact and the knowledge that the Officers have to read their letters "cramps the style" of the men themselves.

On May 23rd an advance guard of 2nd Lieut. Shrive and 14 other ranks proceeded via Southampton to Havre and we did not see them again till arrival at our Battery position in Pommier (a village E. of Doullens) on June 3rd.

The battery transport arrived at Bristol on May 23rd and made a formidable array. It consisted of 33 lorries, 1 motor car (an 18—20 Daimler herein referred to as Mimi) 5 motor cycles, 4 caterpillars and the following personnel 2nd Lieut. Locke, A.S.C. in command, 2nd Lieut. Richardson and 95 other ranks A.S.C. On the same afternoon 2nd Lieut. Locke with 1 N.C.O. and 4 men R.G.A. and 11 men A.S.C. proceeded to Avonmouth to embark, with the guns and transport.

The Battery personnel left Bristol early on May 25th and

proceeded by rail to Paddington, marched to Charing Cross, and left there at noon for Folkestone where we embarked at 5.30 p.m. On arrival at Boulogne we marched to St. Martin's Camp and went under canvas. The journey was carried out without a hitch and exemplified well the splendid working of our transport services. The next four days were spent in completeing clothing and necessaries, sightseeing and learning French. Meanwhile the transport and guns arrived and were parked in the Place Capucine, Boulogne.

Speculation was rife as to what part of the line we were to go to. There had been no extensive operations for some time, but we felt that the Commander-in-Chief would start a big offensive shortly after our arrival. And he did.

On June 1st 1916, we left Boulogne by road, proceeding in the lorries in the direction of Doullens—billetted for the night in the little village of Ruisseauville, 2nd Lieut. Thompson, 2nd Lieut. Locke with 30 R.G.A. and 11 A.S.C. journied by rail with the guns and caterpillars to Doullens.

On June 3rd we marched to our position at Pommier; the store lorries came up at dusk and were unloaded.

While the movement from Boulogne was in progress Mimi, Capt. Kellie and I had gone on in advance to get into touch with our future commanders and select the battery position. We found ourselves allotted to the 19th Group VII Corps, III Army.

CHAPTER II.

POMMIER.

We were all comfortably billetted in the village of Pommier where most of the inhabitants were still in residence, the village having been little damaged by shell fire. (There is not much left of it now.)

During this period detailed orders were given for the carrying out of each operation, and Officers and N.C.O's carefully supervised everything that had to be done. As time went on we gained experience, and before long every man knew what had to be done and how to do it under all conditions. Night work was a new experience to most of us, and there was plenty of it as guns and lorries had to come up after daylight as it was not desirable that we should be spotted by hostile airmen.

The guns were mounted to bear on Gommecourt and the strong German entrenchments to the south of it; they also covered many hostile batteries which were to afford us some sport.

We were busy on June 4th making dug-outs and ammunition recesses when we discovered an old disused well which had been bricked over many years before. The oldest inhabitant knew nothing about it. It was situated 70-ft. in front of No. 2 gun and investigation proved the shaft to be 105-ft. deep, and 5-ft. in diameter, with 5-ft. of water at the bottom. At a depth of 70-ft. two large chambers were discovered from which chalk had been mined in days long gone by. There was room to accomodate the whole battery in these chambers, but they were useless for this purpose being too deep down. However it was decided to utilize the shaft and we started the miners on a job at which they felt very much at home. They descended to a depth of 30-ft. and started a tunnel 6-ft. high and 3-ft. wide from the side of the shaft, running upwards at a slope of 1 in 3 towards the battery, so as to reach the surface between Nos. 1 & 2 guns. The miners worked day and night shifts and the tunnel was completed in three days, most of it being bored through chalk. Removal of the soil was an easy matter as it only had to be dropped to the bottom of the shaft and when this was filled up to the level of the old chambers the soil was moved into them so as not to block the entrances

The tunnel being dug, recesses were constructed leading off it where a B.C. Post, telephone exchange, and accommodation for all personnel were provided at an average depth of 24-ft.

This work took weeks to complete and was by far the safest cover we ever made for ourselves.

On June 8th intimation was received that Capt. Kellie had been awarded the Military Cross for services in 34th S.B.

Our guns came up and were mounted by the 10th June in line with about 30 yards interval between them in a little orchard on the south edge of the village. They were splendidly concealed from air observation and I do not think the Boche ever discovered exactly where we were, though he had a rough idea of our whereabouts, probably from his sound rangers. I flew low over the position one day and I am sure it could never have been spotted unless someone had been lucky enough to see our gun flashes.

It was now apparent that a show of some sort was coming off soon as there were many signs of a coming storm. Other batteries began to arrive stealthily by night and ammunition dumps were largely increased. There was no immediate hurry and we were given plenty of time to prepare our position, but we knew the " show" was going to be a big one as it was evidently to be the result of long and deliberate consideration. Everyone was tremendously eager to do well and to establish a reputation for the Battery. All professed the Regimental Faith quoted by Major J. H. Leslie in his "Tradition in the Royal Regiment of Artillery",—"My Battery is the best in the Brigade ; my subsection is the best in the battery ; and I am the best man in that subsection". No battery commander could wish for a better team of officers than I had, all were thoroughly efficient and absolutely interchangeable, in all the duties that fell to their lot ; and what a happy little family we were! The N.C.O's were practically all regulars, and the rest were the best of the "Kitchener" men, of very high intelligence and magnificent physique. On June 12th we registered all four guns on a point in the German trenches with visual observation from Wagram O.P. This was our first shoot and everything went off perfectly. One round fell bang on an important trench junction and next morning we saw that the Huns had erected a bulls' eye target at this point, facing our lines. This struck me as being of psychological interest as an exhibition of humour from the land of Kultur.

On June 28th we had a stroke of bad luck. All guns were in action when a round from No. 2 sounded abnormally loud, we all looked in its direction and saw that the gun had not "run up" but had remained in the full recoil position. Investigation proved that the shell had exploded in the bore about three feet from the muzzle. This had caused a large egg shaped bulge in the piece and had forced out the sides of the cradle. Of course, one would have expected the gun to have been shattered and resulted in a large number of casualties. A court of enquiry could not fix upon the precise cause of the accident, but it was undoubtedly due to faulty ammunition. The gun and carriage were condemned, and we took one over from 90th S.B.

Our days and nights were busy now improving the battery position, registering many targets, shooting on hostile batteries with aeroplane observation and taking in ammunition, etc. All our shoots went off well and we gained much confidence.

On June 29th Mimi became entitled to her first wounded stripe; she was returning from Hebuterne having dropped the O.P. party there when a shell fell just behind her. A few splinters gave her a war worn appearance and she probably exceeded the speed limit for a little distance otherwise no harm was done.

Towards the end of June it was obvious that "the day" was imminent. The entry in the War Diary for June 26th reads "a very successful days bombardment of front line trenches. Also three excellent counter battery shoots—three batteries being wiped out." A little optimistic perhaps but indicative of the spirit of 91. The next four days were occupied in bombarding the hostile trenches south of Gommecourt and taking on batteries, with great success. Then came July 1st. The plan of attack on our front was to surround the village from north and south. The infantry attack south of the village was at first successful but the troops to the north failed to get going and after a desperate day's fighting our men who had attacked to the south were driven back to their own trenches. What happened further south can be left to historians to tell. We were in action all the day and fired 820 rounds, each shell weighing 290 ℔s.

July 2nd was quiet, but on the 3rd the enemy fired a fair number of shells into our village about a dozen falling just over the battery but without doing any harm. One of these appeared to be a "dud" and we started to dig it out, thereby gaining a little useful experience. Sergt. Kent was in charge of the party and when they had dug about four feet down they found that the shell had burst underground making a cavity about 6-ft. in diameter. A manhole was made into the cavity and Gunner Rabone went down having been told to hold on to Sergt Kent's hand. When he got down he immediately let go and collapsed. Gunner Tagg at once jumped in and with great difficulty raised Rabone so that he could be pulled out. Tagg then collapsed. Bombardier Clarke jumped in but collapsed before he could get Tagg out. Lieuts. Thompson and Shrive then put on their gas helmets and got in and with con-

siderable difficulty got Tagg and Clarke out. The three men and
Sergt. Kent were all unconscious for some time and had been gassed,
and took some days to recover. The cavity was evidently filled with
carbon monoxide gas from the explosion, but it was not a poison
gas shell.

The action of Lieuts. Thompson and Shrive was noteworthy as
there was no certainty that their helmets were proof against the gas.
Their prompt action undoubtedly saved two valuable lives.

After the upheaval of July 1st life quickly settled down to its
normal level in a quiet part of the line. For some days and nights
the enemy continued to drop a few rounds into the village and we
retaliated by shelling his villages and taking on his batteries.

On July 11th we had a stroke of luck.   2nd Lieut. E. B.
Coursey, S.R., joined the battery on posting.

During the intense bombardment of one hour prior to the attack
on July 1st we had been ordered to fire at the rate of 2 rounds per
gun per minute. This was expecting too much from both guns and
gunners and it was now discovered that all the 9·2 equipments re-
quired overhaul by the I.O.M. This was carried out in the battery
position, the guns being put out of action in turn for the purpose.
Orders were issued that 9·2s were not to fire at a greater rate than
one round per minute, and this was extended later to one round per
two minutes. As a matter of fact subsequent experience proved that
they can fire at a rate of one round every 1½ mins., without undue
strain to material or personnel.

Guns had to be put out of action frequently owing to the side
and rear beams shifting in wet soil, resulting in the pickets being
bent. When firing much off the centre line one side of the platform
was liable to sink. It was obvious that the design was far from
perfect and we made many experiments with a view to keeping the
beams from shifting. Eventually the "R.E. Platform" was adopted
by all 9·2 Batteries resulting in greatly increased accuracy of shooting
and considerable saving of labour. These platforms consisted of
three layers of 3″ planks laid under the rear beams and rear ends
of the side beams.

The latter part of July was singularly uneventful and we made
ourselves thoroughly comfortable.

Nine o'clock parade was always held in the battery and all ranks
turned out as smartly as circumstances permitted for roll call and
inspection. The high tone of the battery was largely maintained by
our formal turn out every morning.

On July 27th we started a palatial O.P. in Chiswick Avenue
trench near Hennescamps. We manned this O.P. for the remainder
of our stay at Pommier and I believe it survived for many a day
after we left.

August passed as peacefully as the latter part of July. We
seldom fired a round and got thoroughly bored. Day and night we
could hear the thunder of the guns down south where the great
struggle on the Somme was taking place. We envied our brothers
there and hoped our turn would soon come to take an active part
again.

On August 28th Capt. Kellie proceeded to England to take over command of a Siege Battery—he was a great loss to us. By a curious coincidence he arrived with his new battery six weeks later and took up his position in Bienvillers the nearest village to Pommier where we still were.

Nothing of note occurred till Sept. 13th when we received orders to send one section to Sailly, about 5 miles south of Pommier. Lieuts. Thompson and Coursey accompanied me with the left section and the guns were in action on 14th Sept. Our mission was to take on some hostile batteries with a view to facilitating the attack on Thiepval which was successfully carried out a fortnight later. We had a most satisfactory time and got through a lot of ammunition which was replenished by night. We were firing whenever weather conditions allowed our observation planes to "spot" for us. The battery got considerable "kudos" for its work here and I gratefully acknowledge our debt to Capt. Stanley Clarke, 12th Squadron, R.F.C. who did most of the observation for us; he was one of the most efficient and cheerful airmen we had the pleasure of working with. We always enjoyed counter battery work and later experience convinced me that the 9·2 How. was the best weapon our factories produced for this purpose, owing to its great shell power and accuracy.

During the fortnight we engaged sixteen hostile batteries with uniformly satisfactory results as proved by air photographs taken before and after the shoots. These photos were subsequently forwarded to the Commander-in-Chief who was pleased to express his satisfaction. One particularly pretty little shoot took place on Sept. 23rd; there was a German battery at L.8.b. 90.90. which we took in enfilade. Sixty rounds only were fired and Capt. Stanley Clarke reported it as a "topping shoot". The photos were screened and exhibited at Artillery Schools and elsewhere to show how it should be done.

The Huns indulged in a good deal of desultory shelling of the village by day and night, but never had the luck to do us any harm. We rejoined the right section at Pommier on Oct. 1st. The uninitiated may say "It does not seem reasonable that you could indulge in deliberate destructive shoots on 16 hostile batteries without getting something back." The reply is that our airmen held the air and whenever the Hun planes came to look for us their visit was always a short one and often ended in disaster. Our "Archies" also instilled alarm into the hostile airmen and kept them at a respectful distance. The daring of our pilots and observers was a source of wonder; they used to hover for 1½ to 2 hours over enemy batteries keeping his planes off with their machine guns, dodging his "Archies" and observing and reporting the fall of our rounds. The German airmen had no stomach for this work and when they did try it, it was only in a haphazard fashion. When we rejoined the right section on Oct. 1st we found that they had not been idle, as they had done five quite nice counter battery shoots.

Lieut. C. H. R. Scholefield, our senior subaltern, was appointed Capt. of the Battery vice Kellie. On Oct. 10th Sergt. Odell, No. 1 of No. 2 gun left the battery on receiving a commission. Quiet prevailed till Oct. 17th when we pulled out of our position to move south to join the 5th Army. The weather had been horribly wet for some time, and the night 16-17 Oct. was one of the darkest and wettest I have known. The ground round the guns and ammunition was knee deep in slush and we were all thoroughly "fed up" when we moved off at 5 a.m., on 17th October.

We spent the day at Coinieux and got to our new position at Mailly-Maillet on the night of the 18th Oct. and came under orders of 1st Heavy Artillery Group, V. Corps, V. Army.

No record of our stay at Pommier would be complete without reference to one or two incidents reflecting the lighter side of war. There lived in the village a very dirty and villainous looking French peasant, who was known to the battery as the Pirate. He appeared one day in a clean shirt much to everyone's surprise, and for several days was gloriously drunk and generally created a sensation. Investigations as to his sudden wealth disclosed the fact that he had put in a claim against the battery for 550 francs for alleged damage to the remains of his cottage. He had sold his interest in the claim for 100 francs and was spending the proceeds The claim was not upheld. The rumour that the interest in the claim had been purchased by me is without foundation.

When officers arrived in France they were always strictly enjoined to read General Routine Orders. There was one order directing us to be punctilious about saluting all French Officers that we happened to meet. Lieut. R. S. Scholefield had evidently taken this to heart because he was seen one day smartly saluting the village postman.

CHAPTER III.

BEAUMONT HAMEL AND AFTER.

The weather remained abominable while we got into position in a chalk bank just west of Mailly-Maillet. The registering rounds were fired on Oct. 20th. The chief drawback here was the difficulty of getting ammunition to the guns. Except in dry weather the ammunition lorries could not get nearer to the position than 700 yards so a Decauville railway was constructed and maintained by us over this distance.

We had been sent here to take part in the capture of Beaumont Hamel which closed the Battle of the Somme three weeks later.

Personnel was at first accommodated in the much battered village of Mailly-Maillet, but this was not a health resort and we all moved to the Battery position as dug-outs were constructed. Looking back it is easy to see many ways in which we could have improved our lot, but we still had much to learn from experience. Enthusiasm was at a very high pitch and carried us over the very trying times ahead.

Practically all our work was now directed to the destruction of the enemy's fortified position at Beaumont Hamel and we got very few counter battery shoots. We started straight away on the trenches and strong points in and about where the once beautiful village had been, many rounds being fired daily with O.P. observation and some harrassing rounds by night on communications. On Oct. 23rd we started a daily morning "hate" lasting about ¾ hour commencing at 5 a.m. These morning hates were organised affairs in which all batteries took part and were continued up to the day of attack, Nov. 13th.

One pretty exhibition of Artillery work was given at this period. It was known that the Huns had a very deep and commodious gallery at Beaumont Hamel where they thought they were secure from shell fire. The exact position of the entrances to this gallery was known from air photographs. One night the Bosche was treated to a concentration of gas and shrapnel. As was anticipated large numbers retired underground and we were then turned on to the entrances with a view to blocking them up. The operation was a complete success as proved by inspection of the place after its capture. Some of our sappers opened one of the entrances subsequently and reported that a very large number of Huns had been buried alive.

On Oct. 26th. Lieut. Neilson rejoined the Battery from 19th H.A. Group where he had been employed as signalling officer from 10th August.

On Nov. 2nd while the battery was in action the enemy fired a few H.V. shells at us and one of them ignited a big dump of our cartridges which had just been unloaded 60 yards to the right of the battery. We lost 600 cartridges and about 200 were saved chiefly through the promptitude of Corporal Carrol and Gunner Lock who being near the spot got some men together and started salvage work before the shelling had ceased.

Plenty of ammunition was evidently available now but it was in such odd lots that it gave the officers and B.C.A's endless work in making the necessary calculations. Each of the four guns had a different muzzle velocity with any given nature of charge and shell. We were now getting two natures of propellant, viz. cordite and N.C.T. giving different m.vs. according to the state of the wear of the guns. We discovered that with new guns the gas check and vavassour driving bands ranged about the same, but as the guns became worn the difference in range increased rapidly, the gas check going further than the vavassour. In one shoot that we carried out later in Belgium two guns were employed one being quite new and the other very much worn; both were firing vavassour driving bands at a range of about 8,700 yards and the difference in elevation between them was 11 degrees, representing about 750 yards range. I am speaking from memory but am sure about the 11 degrees. Any gunner will realise how necessary it was to make careful and rapid calculations, and how difficult it was to do so, often under circumstances of great discomfort and in the intervals of precarious slumber. The uniform good shooting of the battery was largely due to the efficient work of our admirable B.C.A's.

Our bombardment of the enemy's position by day and night continued up to the morning of 13th November when our infantry went over behind the best barrage they had seen up to that time. All went well, but the enemy delivered many counter attacks and fought with great stubbornness for some days, before he finally accepted defeat and left us in possession of this very important position. I can best convey an idea of the work done during these few days by quoting the War Diary as it stands :—.

"*Nov. 13th*. The attack on Beaumont Hamel opened at "5.45 a.m. The battery was in action throughout the day "supporting the infantry by a series of barrages. No. 1 gun "went out of action owing to broken firing beams. A/Bombdr. "A. White one of by B.C.A's and Pte. Allardyce, R.F.C. the "battery wireless operator were killed by a shell in Mailly-"Maillet. Sergt. W. G. Taylor (No. 1 of No. 3 gun) proceeded "to join III Army on being appointed to a commission."

"*Nov. 14th*. The battery has now been in continuous action "for 28½ hours and is still in action. Severe fighting is still "going on E. of Beaumont Hamel. The detachments are very "tired but very cheerful. Ammunition has had to be conveyed "to the battery along 700 yards of Decauville railway, this gives "no time for rest. No. 1 gun in action again on a new platform. "The battery remained in action all day, firing at rates varying "from 1 round per gun per minute to 10 rounds per hour.

"*Nov. 15th*. Battery continued in action all day. During "the afternoon a fatigue party of 20 infantry arrived to assist "with shell fatigues. Severe fighting continued on our front."

"*Nov. 16th*. Battery continued in action till 3.25 p.m. "when there was a short pause ; thus the guns were firing con-"tinuously for 81 hours and 40 minutes."

"*Nov. 17th*. Firing continued throughout the day ; there "have only been two short pauses of less than half an hour "since 5.45 a.m. on the 13th. At about 4 p.m. the breech of "No. 2 gun blew out killing Corpl. Clemans the No. 1, and "Gunners Ritchie and Whiting. Lieut. Coursey the section "commander was wounded."

"*Nov. 18th*. Battery continuously in action all day."

"*Nov. 19th*. Early in the day No. 4 gun was put out of "action by damaged side beams and during the afternoon No. 1 "gun was put out of action from the same sause. No. 3 gun "still in action without a hitch. At 11 p.m. Nos. 2 and 4 guns "reported ready for action."

"*Nov. 20th*. Bombardment at a slow rate continued through "the day."

"*Nov. 21st*. Same as yesterday."

"*Nov. 22nd*. At 8 a.m. No. 3 gun reported out of action "owing to broken side beams. This gun was in action, except "for the two short pauses already mentioned for 10 days 2¼ "hours. After No. 3 was put out of action, only Nos. 2 and 4 "remained. At 4 p.m. 'Cease firing' was ordered, the battery "having been in action at various rates for 10 days 10¼ hours "save for the two pauses. The strain on the equipment had "been very severe and all the platforms and earth boxes are "badly damaged."

The War Diary makes no comment on the strain on the personnel. What little rest and food the men got during those ten days was enjoyed in the mud beside the guns. A feeble cheer greeted the order to " Cease Fire".

The latter end of November was fairly quiet. We shelled Munich Trench, N. of Beaumont Hamel and carried out occassional short bombardments of Pusieux in retalliation for the shelling of our villages. We always sent back much more than we got.

On December 1st we celebrated our first birthday. Lieut. Coursey returned, having recovered from his wound.

The blowing out of the breech of No. 2 gun was investigated, but no definite conclusion was formed as to its cause. A change of target had been ordered when the gun was loaded with a full charge round. It was necessary to fire a reduced charge at the new target and the No. 2 was opening the breech to take out the full charge, when it went off for some unknown reason. At the moment of the explosion only the two front threads of the breech screw were engaged in the breech as they were shorn off. The block was blown about 500 yards to the rear of the gun and the shell remained firmly wedged in the bore about four feet from the muzzle and refused to be moved by any mechanical means that could be devised. The fuze was removed by a courageous I.O.M. and after much cogitation it was decided to fire the shell out. It could not be fired towards Hunland as it would probably not go as far and would fall in our own lines. Finally we were ordered to take the gun to the rear, mount it opposite a steep hill and fire the shell into it. All preparations were solemnly made and the gun was loaded with the lowest charge. No experts could tell us what would happen and it was thought quite likely that the gun would burst, so it was fired with a lanyard 50 yards long by a man in a dug-out. The tube went off all right, but we heard nothing else. All thought it was a misfire and Sergt Kent went to extract the tube. As soon as he turned it, it flew out of the vent with great force and a loud hissing noise commenced lasting for ten minutes. The charge had fired noiselessly being confined and had failed to propel the shell. The hissing noise was caused by the escape of the gas through the vent. The experiment was repeated with 2nd charge and gave a similar result. It was then decided to try a full charge which drove the shell into the hill and did no damage whatever to the gun, which was used for a long time afterwards.

During December our activity was confined to retaliation on the enemy villages and " crumping" trenches occassionally. Our special attention was directed to Munich trench. Our infantry set out to capture this one day but couldn't find it.

On Dec. 13th we were detailed to find a working party of 120 men to construct a cable trench to Continental O.P. on Schwaben Redoubt. They were billetted in Aveuly Wood where they had an uncomfortable time in bad dug-outs and very cold weather. There were also many well founded complaints about the rations. This party rejoined the battery on December 24th. On December 18th Capt. Scholefield was attached to 15th Squadron, R.F.C. for a week, and Lieut. Neilson went on a signalling course.

Christmas Day was celebrated with the aid of a little extra provender collected by Mimi in Amiens and we fired three salvos at the Huns' billets during their meal times.

On December 27th B.S.M. Newton left the battery on discharge after 36 years service, aged 56. He was a very fine old soldier, and the smartness of the battery was very largely due to him. I always gave him full marks for style on parade and it was quite a treat to see him calling the battery to attention and collecting reports at 9 o'clock every morning.

On December 31st Lieut. Neilson rejoined.

The winter was intensely cold with a great deal of snow. The temperature on two or three occassions going below zero. We made one curious discovery with regard to the shooting of the guns in this intense cold. They always shot short unless a larger allowance was made for temperature, than that given by the range table. When the temperature was above, about 40 degrees, the range table figures held good, but below this an increasing allowance had to be made as the temperature fell. At zero, the allowance was as much as two degrees at long ranges. The column in the range table giving the difference in range caused by a variation of 10 degrees temperature from normal requires revision for temperature below 40 degrees.

The New Year was issued in uneventfully; the weather continuing to be very cold and dry. On January 5th we started in earnest on Munich Trench. This ran along the crest of a ridge north of Beaumont Hamel and had considerable tactical value, so the powers that were decided to capture it. On the 5th we fired 45 rounds on the trench and dug-outs east of it, on the 6th 100 rounds, on the 7th 50 rounds, on the 8th 240 rounds, on the 9th 200 rounds. On the 10th we started a bombardment of 24 hours during which we fired 640 rounds. At dawn on the 11th our troops advanced against the trench but were somewhat bewildered by the fact that the trench was not to be found, (as previously stated). They succeeded however in digging themselves in where it had been. At 3 p.m. we started a bombardment of the dug-outs, etc. E. of our new line which lasted till 8 a.m. the following day.

On 15th 2nd Lieut. Page, R.M.A. was attached to the battery for two weeks. He learnt most that there was to know about 9·2 Hows. and contributed largely to the enjoyment of life in the officers mess. He could pull his own leg as well as anyone I know.

On the 16th, 17th and 18th we were busy bombarding Glory Lane and enemy headquarters in L 33, in support of an attack by the IV Corps.

The front lines on both sides were very ill defined on our front at this period, and consisted of lines of fortified shell-holes. Our infantry did a certain amount of nibbling and there was some very dirty fighting at Ten Tree Alley. On the 23rd we fired 150 rounds on Pendant Alley West after a good registration by aeroplane. On the 24th I went on ten days leave. There is nothing of interest to record for the latter part of January.

On February 2nd, Capt. Scholefield proceeded to England for a B.C's course. On the 3rd and 4th February we carried out a bombardment in support of an attack by the 11th Corps on Puisieux and

River Trenches. On the 10th February we started work on a proposed new position in Station Road, Beaumont Hamel. We expended much labour on this position but were not destined to occupy it.

The battery was withdrawn from the line on February 15th for a much needed rest. We had not been out of the line since June 1916. We had to leave behind two officers and 43 men to continue work on the new position and to find guards for the guns, storemen, cooks, etc. This party had a hard time, as they were called upon to do a considerable amount of shooting which we had not been led to anticipate and consequently did not allow for. Lieuts. Thompson and Shrive remained behind and Lieuts. Neilson and Coursey accompanied me with the main body. We spent our period of rest at Drucat near Abbeville far from the tumult of war and all entered into the spirit of the occasion by making it a real rest. The only parades were the daily roll call and inspection at 9 a.m. Abbeville was within walking distance, and in spite of the allurements of a large town there was a remarkable absence of crime and 91 maintained its discipline and tone.

One day while we were on rest the glad news came that the enemy had retired on our front evacuating Serre Puisieux and other villages. This was in fact the Huns' strategic retirement to the Hindenburg line which is a matter of history, Meanwhile the party left with the guns was kept busy firing with very much reduced detachments on the retiring enemy and supporting our advance which was keenly contested. The main body returned to Mailly Maillet on March 1st to find that the enemy had retired out of range and we set to and dismounted the guns.

On 2nd March, Capt. Scholefield returned from B.C's course and leave.

On 3rd, 2nd Lieut. Coursey and 20 men went to Beaumont Hamel and continued work on the position in Station Road. A period of suspense ensued while the powers above decided on our next move. On March 20th, we received orders to transfer half the battery to Beauval (behind the lines). Accordingly the right section, under Lieuts. Neilson, Coursey, Shrive and myself moved off on 21st March. We proceeded via Beauval, St. Michel, Tingues to St. Catherines (a suburb of Arras) where we arrived on 24th March.

The left section under Capt. Schoefield and Lieut. Thompson remained at Mailly Maillet till 30th March when they started on their iourney to ioin the Battery Headquarters.

CHAPTER IV.

ARRAS AND MESSINES.

When we arrived at St. Catherines we found ourselves allotted to 83rd Brigade, 17th Corps. The right section guns were mounted on 26th March.

On March 27th our old friend Capt. Kellie turned up to be

attached to the battery.   He had since we last saw him become an instructor at the III Army Artillery School.

It was pretty obvious that we were in for another big show. Our first important shoot was on the 29th March when we fired 150 rounds on cutting wire with the new 106 fuse.   The enemy artillery began to get aggressive and on the 31st they put two 5·9's in our position, one just outside each flank of the line of guns.   It looked as if they had us nicely " taped."

On April 2nd the left section rejoined and their guns were immediately mounted.

On April 3rd, Gunner Gosling was wounded by a splinter in the battery position and was evacuated. On April 4th Capt. Kellie was in the house in Arras which was occupied as our officers mess when the front wall was blown in by a shell.   He wore a piece of plaster on his head for a few days and his steel helmet was not very comfortable.   This was "V" day of the battle of Arras and we engaged a hostile battery and numerous strong points in the enemy's defences. April 5th " W" day, we did two excellent destructive counter battery shoots.   We had a bit of bad luck this day ; a gas shell burst in the battery office and resulted in B.S.M. Baker, C., B.Q.M.S. Castle, Sergt. Mescal, (our irreproachable pay sergt.) Gunner Walker and A/Bombardier Brown being evacuated to hospital.   A/Bombardier Brown one of the most excellent men in the battery died from gas poisoning next day.   It was an unpleasant experience to have the whole battery staff laid low on the eve of a battle and something had to be done.   Sergt. Baker G. the No. 1 of No. 4 gun stepped into the breach and combined the duties of B.S.M., B.Q.M.S. and pay sergt. and carried on without a hitch.

April 6th, " X" day we amused ourselves wire-cutting and taking on machine gun emplacements.   April 7th, " Q" day we did some more bombardment and calibrated our pieces with some new charges of M.D.T. that had been sent up.   To add to our troubles it was found that the M.D.T. shot much below range table m.v. Gunner McMullen was wounded by a splinter in the battery.   April 8th "Y" day we engaged a hostile battery with 100 rounds and bombarded six strong points.   April 9th "Z" day marked one of the big achievements of British arms during the war.   All objectives were captured including the famous Vimy Ridge.   I will always remember the advance of the Canadians against the village of Thelus on the ridge which they took at the point of the bayonet.   Sergt. Green the battery signalling Sergt. had been detailed to go forward with the attacking infantry and lay a line to the " Pont du jour" where we were to establish an O.P.   In carrying out his duties he came upon an abandoned 4·2 How.   He assisted two R.G.A. officers to turn this piece on the retiring Huns who offered an excellent target at a very short range over the open sights.   They got off some 30 rounds with excellent effect before being compelled to desist owing to the attentions of a 5·9″ battery which got right on to them.

The O.P.'s used by us during the battle were a house on the E. edge of Arras and the Semenaire.

On the 10th I visited the German gun positions that we had engaged and found that in every case all the pits had been destroyed and shattered guns remained in many of the pits. We cannot claim all the credit for this as other batteries had engaged the same targets, but there was no doubt that most of the havoc had been wrought by 9·2's.

During the ensuing week we had little to do and as danger from a serious counter attack disappeared our guns were dismounted.

On April 16th the left section was ordered to advance to Rocqulencourt and came under the 13th Corps, but still remained in 83 Brigade. On the 18th the right section joined the left. On the 19th we silenced an active hostile battery with visual observation and shelled Gavrelle. Gunner Constable was wounded by a stray bullet fired by someone behind our lines. The 20th and 21st and 22nd were spent in shelling trenches in B.30 and C.25. On the latter date Gunner Palmer was wounded while repairing the O.P. line. On the 23rd we assisted in the protection barrage for our attack on, and capture of Gavrelle.

We had been ordered to get a couple of guns into position at B.25d.8.2. north of the Bailleul-Arras road. This represented an advance of about two miles over shell-pitted roads impassible to lorries. Lieut. Shrive dismounted No. 2 gun at 10 p.m. on the 22nd and reported the gun in action at the new position at 5 a.m. on the 23rd. I could hardly believe him but the feat had been accomplished with one caterpillar, a couple of hand carts and some stout hearts. On the 24th No. 1 gun joined No. 2 at the B.25.d. position and the lines of both guns were registered. A very nice C.B. shoot was carried out by the right section on the 26th against a battery at C.28.a.5.6. On the 27th the left section joined the right, we carried out a 'blind' C.B. shoot and fired 20 rounds on S.O.S. targets.

We fired 600 rounds on the 28th in support of our attack on Oppy. On the 29th No. 4 gun had to be remounted owing to tilt and we carried out two small bombardments on C.29.3.8.5.

The 30th was fairly quiet.

Considerable activity was maintained during the first fortnight of May, and I will quote the War Diary.

"1st May. 20 rounds at C.15.c.37.38. Fifty rounds at Masville Farm with visual observation ; farm buildings demolished."

"2nd May. Twenty rounds each at C.15.c.44 and C.15.c.8.5."

"3rd May. Infantry attacked Oppy again at 4 a.m. Fired about 300 rounds at active hostile batteries."

"4th May. 120 rounds aeroplane shoot on a.h.b. at C.15.a.O.6. 8 O.K's."

"5th May. Fairly quiet."

"6th May. Our position shelled by 150ᵐ/ᵐ h.v. gun. About 30 rounds one of which blew up 270 cartiridges. 2nd Lieut. Rumball temporarily attached to the battery."

"7th May. 150 rounds on a.h.b. at C.23.c.25.15 first 28 rounds observed by aeroplane, ranging quite satisfactory. Twenty rounds at C.27.c.20.80. Battery again shelled by h.v. gun."

"8th May. 35 rounds fired to silence a.h.b.s."

"9th May. 95 rounds neutralisation fired. 150 rounds with aeroplane observation on a battery at C.15.c.85.30. Successful."

"10th May. 100 rounds on a.h.b. at C.27.c.20.75. Successful."
"11th May. 35 rounds neutralisation on C.28.b.85.95 and
C.22.b.29.20 During this shoot Nos. 2 and 3 guns remained in
action under heavy shelling by 150$^{m/m}$ h.v. guns. Ten rounds fell
within 50 yards of the guns. All ranks showed great gallantry and
the service of the guns was uninterrupted."
"12th May. A good shoot of 100 rounds observed by aeroplane
on a.h.b. at C.25.c.75.15."

Our next big battle during the spring offensive of 1917 was now
in course of preparation and on the 13th May the right section pulled
out to Mareuil en route to the Second Army Area under Lieuts
Nielson, Coursey and myself. We rested here till the 18th when
we moved to Brouay, on the 19th we went to Bailleul, and on the
20th came into position at T.15.d.4.5 on the outskirts of Neuve
Eglise. The left section joined us a couple of days later, we came
under the 11th H.A.G.

On the 23rd and 24th May we fired on Messines and a trench
near it with visual observation.

May 25th was the anniversary of our arrival in France. During
the year the battery had served under the following commands :—
19th H.A.G. 7th Corps, III Army, from June 1st 1916 to Oct. 17th
1916, taking part in the attack on Gommecourt on July 1st and the
attack on Thiepval in Sept. 1st H.A.G. 5th Corps, V Army from
17th October 1916 to 21st March 1917, taking part in the capture of
Beaumont Hamel on 13th November and the operations on the Ancre
during the winter preceding the enemy's retirement. 83rd H.A.G.
17th Corps, III Army from March 24th to April 14th taking part in
the battle of Arras. 83rd H.A.G. 13th Corps, I Army from April
14th to May 13th, taking part in the capture of Gavrelle and the
operations at Oppy and Fresnoy. 11th H.A.G. 2nd Anzac Corps,
II Army, 20th May to 24 May on which date the 49th H.A.G. took
over from the 11th H.A.G.

We were destined to serve for many months in 49 H.A.G. and
a very happy time we had with them. The Colonel was a very
gallant soldier who earned the respect of all of us. He was very
exacting at times but always just, he thoroughly understood 91,
encouraged the spirit that was there, and got the best out of us.

On May 26th we fired 80 rounds with aeroplane observation, the
pilots remark on this was—"The best shoot I have seen!" The same
target got 80 rounds on the following day.

On the 29th we fired 60 rounds on a trench from O.32.a.85.20
to 79.33. with visual observation and good results.

The 30th was moderately quiet and on 31st 150 rounds were
fired at Ontario trench with visual observation ; most of the trench
was obliterated. On June 1st we fired 100 rounds on a trench
running from O.32.b.84.70 to 65.75 and 20 rounds at O.31.b.4.20.
The enemy was beginning to take notice of the activity on our front
and began a certain amount of desultory shelling. We were frequently treated during the day to a small ration of 4·2's in the vicinity of
our billets and guns. By night a few gas shell used to interrupt cur
slumbers. Neuve Eglise station where we had to handle a large
amount of ammunition received attention from 5·9's.

This was the first time I had noticed the enemy using an instantaneous fuze. Some of the 4·2s bursting near the billets made very small craters, and the fragments were projected radially at right angles to the axis of the shell. They were nasty dangerous things and caused many casualties.

June 2nd was "V" day of the attack on Messines Ridge; we fired 30 rounds at U.2.b.93.65 and 75 rounds at U.2.b.92.85 to 82.85. These were trench targets.

June 3rd. We fired 30 rounds at Wychaate village, 25 rounds at Messines and 400 rounds on a trench from U.9.a.82.55 to U.9.b. 23.50 with aeroplane observation and excellent effect. A few shells burst near the guns.

June 4th "W" day; we fired 400 rounds with aeroplane observation on a trench from O.32.b.08.85 to 25.5 very good results. Messines received 30 rounds and O.31.b.85.65 got 145. More shells fell near the battery on this day.

June 5th. "X" day. We fired 70 rounds at a hostile battery at O.33.b.60.60. Aeroplane observation, and 55 rounds at a "pill box" at O.31.o.85.65. During the afternoon shells fell near the men's bivouacs and officers' mess causing the following casualties: Gunner E. Ogle, killed. B.S.M. H. C. Fish (who had joined us about three weeks previously) B.Q.M.S. G. Baker (who had been just promoted) Gunner H. S. Jones, Gunner F. Gray, and Gunner G. E. Slkovsky, were all slightly wounded and returned to duty. June 6th "Y" day. 200 rounds "blind" and 200 rounds with aeroplane at U.8.a.10.80 very good results. Gunners F. E. Maslen and W. Whysche were slightly wounded and returned to duty.

June 7th "Z" day. Messines Ridge and all objectives captured. The battery carried out a detailed programme, firing many hundreds of rounds from 3.10 a.m. to 7.50 p.m. Most of the shooting was on active hostile batteries and N.F. calls.

June 8th. We fired 80 rounds at O.34.b.35.90 to 71.30 and 140 rounds at O.35 central.

June 9th. The left section advanced and came into action at T.12.g.22.52 near Wulvergem.

June 10th. The right section advanced and came into position at T.11.b.71.32. The left section moved into position alongside the right section as a railway 12″ How. had come up and wanted to fire directly over them. Leave started on this day for N.C.O's and men, the battery allotment being one or two leaves per day.

June 11th and 12th were fairly uneventful; on the 13th we fired 135 rounds at Sunken Farm and 25 rounds on O.12.a.38.83 with aeroplane. June 14th, 150 rounds fired on U.17.a.50.oo, 45 rounds on V.2.a.oo.94. Bombardier Robinson was wounded through the explosion of a R.F.A. ammunition dump near the position. There was a concentration of batteries round us at this time and during the next few days we came in for some desultory shelling.

June 15th. We fired 160 rounds on P.31.a.40.80 and 20 rounds on P.32 c.23.32 both with aeroplane and 20 rounds on Mai-Cornet.

June 16th. Twenty rounds fired at Mai-Cornet and 12 rounds registration at Chateau Ghesquiere.

June 17th. Fired 100 rounds at some houses at V.2.b.2.1. and V.2.d.1.2. aeroplane observation and good results. Also 300 rounds at a.h.b. at V.3.c.oo.45, very successful. Gunner Roche was slightly wounded and returned to duty.

June 18th. 30 rounds with balloon observation at V.3.a.1.7 moderate results.

June 19th was fairly quiet, and on the 20th the battery position and vicinity was shelled with 5·9 from 3 p.m. to 7.30 p,m., no damage or casualties.

June 21st. Fired 15 rounds with visual observation on a.h.b. in V.7.a. Gunners Hodgkinson and Sills wounded by splinters in the battery. Gunner Young, A. V. evacuated for exhaustion. Lieut. Neilson went on leave.

June 22nd was fairly quiet. On 23rd we silenced an a.h.b. in V.14.c. with visual observation. 120 5·9s fell in or near the battery.

On June 24th the battery pulled out of position and went for three days rest to Bailleul; on the 27th we moved to St. Marie Capelle (near Cassel), on the 28th we went to Wormhout and on the 29th to La Panne and came under XV Corps; 49th H.A.G. had also moved up north and we remained with it.

I have already referred to the occasion on which the officers mess in Arras was blown in by a shell. One little incident occurred in connection with this which impressed itself on my memory. When the shell arrived all occupants of the premises made a frantic rush for the cellar. Ten seconds later the mess waiter remembered that a bottle of whiskey had been left on the mess table, and he immediately went up to see that it was safe. He rushed upstairs only just in time to see the whiskey vanishing through the crump hole in the wall. Some Scotchmen were billetted next door. Time from crump to vanishing of whiskey—20 seconds.

CHAPTER V.

BELGIUM.

As the nature of the country and the conditions for fighting differed considerably from those existing on other parts of the front, a short description of our surroundings will not be out of place here.

Our position was at Groot Westhoff Farm situated about 1½ miles west of the village of Pervyse which was just behind our front line. The country was flat all round as far as the eye could see except for the sand dunes on the coast near Nieuport which was about seven miles north of us. The front lines were barricades separated by the flooded area along the course of the river Yser. Villages and farms surrounded by a few trees dotted the landscape. The country was intersected by numerous dykes and canals by which it was drained. A good road ran westward from Pervyse to Furnes and our farm was ½ mile north of this road. Suitable positions for guns were very few and far between as water was within three feet of the surface of the ground. Ordinary dug-outs could not be constructed and all protective cover had to be built up.

In one way it was a siege gunner's paradise because it was impossible to screen gun flashes in the dead flat country, and both sides indulged in cross observations. British troops had just taken over the line on the coast at Nieuport from the French; but the line immediately in front of us was held by the Belgian Army, our rôle being to engage the German batteries which more or less enfiladed our troops on the coast. So the 49th H.A.G. found themselves isolated on the Belgian area. We at once struck up an entente, and made many valued friends among our Allies; the more we saw of them the better we liked them. For the Belgian gunners in particular we had the highest admiration; they applied the science and practice of gunnery with vivid imagination which must have been very annoying to our enemies. Had they been supplied with more and better guns the Belgian Artillery would have been second to none.

The provision of O.P's was a difficult problem and we selected a ruined house in Pervyse. Naturally the Belgian gunners had occupied all the best O.P's which made an entente all the more desirable. Major A. Wery (who was awarded the D.S.O. later for the services he rendered us) commanded the local group of Belgian Heavy Artillery. He and his staff were most charming and hospitable to us, and did much to make this our happiest time during the war. With his help I got an excellent scheme in working order whereby we did the shooting and the Belgians did the observation. I used to go to his headquarters and fight the battery by telephone from there; the cross observations coming in direct from the O.P's. In this manner we did some very satisfactory shoots. The O.P's could see many of the hostile gun flashes and had them all carefully registered. If we wanted to shoot on any particular emplacement the observation instruments could be clamped on it immediately. There were a few little difficulties which were soon overcome such as the difference between the British and Belgian system of map squares; observations sent in milliemes were easily converted into degrees and minutes.

Most of our shoots were done with aeroplane observation and we had the aid of 52nd Squadron which included some admirable pilots. Chief amongst these were Lieuts Rogers and Donaldson. The former of these gallant officers unfortunately met his end under dramatic circumstances. He had a fight with a hostile scout one day during which he was hit in the thigh with a phosphorous bullet. He drove the Hun off and then flew his machine straight to one of our hospitals where he made a good landing. He was taken out unconscious and died shortly afterwards.

It was intended to carry out an attack on the German position on the coast about the middle of July. The enemy however anticipated this by a local attack, which was very well executed on July 10th and our plans were abandoned. The enemy had a strong concentration of artillery in front of us, many of his guns being in concrete covered emplacements and it was decided to engage some of them.

The British troops in this area had come under command of the 4th Army.

We got into position at Groot Westhoff Farm on the night 4th—5th July. We were to remain silent till the opening of the proposed British attack, and did so till the German attack on July 10th. On this day we were turned on to neutralize two hostile batteries. Just after we had ceased fire at 9.20 p.m. the enemy opened on us with a 150$^{m/m}$ gun battery. Sixty rounds were fired. Sergt. B. Carrol who had been promoted the same day was killed. Seven gun wheels and one carriage transporting gun were damaged. Sergt. Carrol was a splendid N.C.O. and one of the most popular men in the battery. He had previously served under me in 34th Siege Battery and in the British Legation Guard Pekin before the war.

On July 11th we fired 85 rounds neutralization on various batteries. After we had ceased fire the enemy opened on us again with a 150$^{m/m}$ gun battery, from 6.30 p.m. to 9.30 p.m. 230 rounos were fired, casualties nil, damage to materiel—one wheel destroyed and most of our small stores buried under the ruins of the farm buildings.

July 12th. Fired 10 rounds neutralization at TX3 and TX4. (active hostile batteries.)

July 13th. Did a 200 round aeroplane shoot on TX4. Excellent results, three of the four pits being destroyed. This was the battery which had shelled us. Received a ration of ten 4·2s during the evening, no harm done.

July 14th. From 6 p.m. to 8.30 p.m. we were heavily shelled with 5·9s and 4·2s. All our guns were put out of action. No. 1 gun had the earth box destroyed and carriage and sight damaged, and could not be repaired in the battery. No. 2's earth box was destroyed. No. 3 had its earth box and platform damaged, also its carriage transporting gun. No. 4's platform was damaged. Many small stores were damaged and missing.

This was a nasty blow, but not a knock out. Our position was a mass of muddy shell holes rendering the moving of our heavy pieces a difficult operation. We tackled the job straight away and by piecing odd bits together we got Nos. 2 and 4 gun in action by dawn on the 15th. We however got orders to move the guns before firing again. Consequently we moved them forward 100 yards and had them ready for action at dawn on 16th. We fired a few rounds on the 17th at N.3.a.6.5 without observation. The 16th, 17th and 18th were chiefly devoted to re-laying our Decauville railway, getting up ammunition, and making cover for the personnel. By this time we had got the hang of the situation and realised that we were up against something, so made up our minds and our plans acocrdingly. All accommodation was kept to a flank as far as possible and scattered. Not more than three or four men slept in one shelter; ammunition was kept in small lots. The men were instructed as to where they should go in case of hostile shelling if they were not on the guns. In fact we did all possible to prepare for eventualities. The spirit of 91 was never more in evidence than at this time, and our superiors did everything to encourage it. Our Brigade helped us in every way; we were frequently visited by Brig.-Genl. Collingwood, commanding the 15th Corps Heavy Artillery and twice we had the honour of being visited by the Army Commander, Genl. Sir Henry Rawlinson. On each occasion he spoke to the men in terms of appreciation and encouragement nothing could have helped them more to carry on.

To return to details:—On 19th July we fired 40 rounds with aeroplane observation, on TX4 getting five O.K's.

July 20th. Fired 6 rounds unobserved at TX3. This was a very aggressive anti-aircraft battery of large calibre in concrete emplacements. Also fired 140 rounds at TX4 getting 12 O.K's this was the end of our friend TX4. TX1 received 105 rounds with very good results. On July 21st we fired 10 rounds at TX6 and 30 rounds at TX2 aeroplane observation, fair results. We were shelled from 4 p.m. to 7 p.m. with about 20 rounds of 5·9. A lorry full of shells was blown up and some cartridges ignited.

July 22nd. Fired 270 rounds at TX6; an excellent shoot including 15 O.Ks; 65 rounds fired during the night on S.O.S. lines.

July 24th. Fired 360 rounds at NZ14,—8 O.Ks. We were again crumped with 250 5·9s from 4 p.m. to 8 p.m. No. 1 gun's carriage, transporting, was badly damaged, some shells and cartridges were blown up, and the farm buildings burned down. We were suffering a good deal of damage at this time, small repairs were carried out in the battery by our most praiseworthy Staff-Sergt. Artificer Negus, and the bigger jobs were taken in hand by No. 4 Heavy Mobile Workshop, under Major Morris, M.C. without whose aid we could not possibly have kept our end up. We threw a heavy strain on this officer and his staff, and nothing could excel the despatch and efficiency with which they carried out their work. ₍

On July 25th, eighty rounds were fired at NY12—5 O.Ks. We were shelled from 1 p.m. to 7 p.m. by 5·9 Hows., 300 rounds. No 1 gun carriage badly damaged, and No. 2's earth box destroyed. This left us with only No. 4 in action but during the night a new earth box was put on No. 2.

On July 26th we fired 20 rounds "blind" at TX7 and TX8; also 165 rounds at TX7 with aeroplane observation and excellent results. During the night we fired on S.O.S. lines and "harrassed" TX7 with 40 rounds. 2nd Lieut. J. L. Plumbridge joined us about this date.

July 27th. We received about 10 rounds from a small calibre gun. We fired 20 rounds without observation on TX7, 20 rounds with visual observation on NZ10, 75 rounds on TX7 and 65 rounds on TX8; these last two with aeroplane observation and excellent results. During the night the enemy treated us to three bursts of harassing fire.

On July 28th, to the great regret of all Lieut. Neilson left us on being posted as second in command of 203 Siege Battery. We fired 105 rounds with aeroplane observation on TX11—6 O.Ks. We were "harassed" during the day with about 50 rounds from a small h.v. gun. During the night we fired on S.O.S. lines and "harassed" TX11 and TX7.

On July 29th we fired 100 rounds at NY8 after ranging visually on a datum point. About 50 rounds fired at us by a small h.v. gun. We harrassed TX1 and TX14 with 30 rounds during the night.

On July 30th we fired 40 rounds "blind" at TX1 and TX14. We were "straffed" by 5'9 Hows. from 4 p.m. to 9 p.m. 300 rounds were fired. Both guns were put out of action. No. 2 owing to damaged carriage, earth box and beams, and No. 4 owing to damaged carriage and breech. Many stores, wheels, etc. were lost or damaged. This was a bad ending to a very entertaining three weeks during which we had undoubtedly inflicted a great deal more damage than we received. These hostile shoots were not observed by aeroplane, but from the ground or balloons. It was impossible to conceal our gun flashes which reached up to 40 feet when firing at high elevations. We tried screens of canvas but could not get them high enough, without being horribly conspicuous. Smoke screens were also largely employed by us, and undoubtedly saved us to a certain extent but they were more useful in preventing the enemy from observing his own shell bursts than in concealing our flashes.

We now chose a new position behind a hedge, about 100 yards in advance of our last, for the right section; here No. 1 gun was mounted on August 1st and No. 2 on August 2nd. The weather during the first six days of August was very bad, no observation was possible; so we devoted our energies to repairing damages and replacing our lost stores. All ranks kept in excellent health and spirits.

I have often been asked how it was that we did not suffer more casualties to personnel. It was due to luck and good management. The chief reason was that we carried out our destructive shoots in the morning, the light being better for aeroplane observation, while the enemy chose the afternoon. This used to interfere with our evening meal as we used to clear out of the position and the cook-house seemed to have fatal attraction for hostile shells. We had some enterprising battery cooks who rose to the occasion. There was a canal running east and west alongside the position; on this canal, they found an old disused small barge about 20 ft. long. This they converted into a mobile cook-house. Its normal position was near the guns but when things became very unpleasant it was paddled some 300 or 400 yards to the rear, where we all assembled, had tea, and watched the fireworks. We fixed up a tapping-in station also to the rear whence we were in communication all round.

Although we had two guns in action again on the 2nd August we did not fire. On the 5th, 30 rounds were fired without observation at TX11 and NZ13. On the 6th TX5 and NZ14 were similarly treated to 30 rounds. On August 7th the visibility improved and we fired 25 rounds to datum. 25 rounds at TX5 and 30 rounds at TX7 and NZ14. Twenty-five shells of small calibre fell in the position. On this date Lieuts. R. Shrive and E. B. Coursey received the Military Cross.

August 8th. We fired 50 rounds at NZ14 and TX7, 10 rounds at NZ16, 40 rounds at TX9 and NZ15.

August 9th. Fired 150 rounds at NZ13—9 O.Ks, and 40 rounds during the night at TX9 and NZ14.

August 10th. Fired 120 rounds at TX9, the first 50 being observed by aeroplane and the remainder " blind"; also 120 rounds at TX1—7 O.K's and 100 rounds at T-X11 with cross observation from our O.P's with good results. Thirty small shells were fired to neutralize us, but they did not.

August 11th. Eighty-five rounds fired at TX7 observed by Belgian O.P's—satisfactory; also 120 rounds at NY12—2 O.K's and 13 Y's. About 100 5·9s and 4·2s fired at us—no harm done.

August 12th. Fired 185 rounds at NZ13—9 O.Ks. We were crumped during the afternoon with 150 5·9s and during the night with 50 4·2s. No damage done.

August 13th. Fired 15 rounds into the village of Mannekensvere and 60 rounds at TX9 with Belgian observation. Satisfactory. An explosion and fire were caused.

August 14th. We fired eigth rounds at NZ13 and TX1, 10 rounds at Nieuwiendamme fort and 70 rounds at TX7. 10.K. Also 100 rounds unobserved at TX11. Twenty small h.v. shells in the battery.

August 15th. We fired 100 rounds at NY12—5 O.Ks and 100 rounds unobserved at TX11.

August 16th. Fired 135 rounds at TX1—3 O.Ks and 30 Ys, 100 rounds at NZ13—3 O.Ks and 5 Ys. Also 100 rounds without observation at TX15.

August 17th. Nos. 3 and 4 guns had now been repaired and were mounted in a new position in an open field abaut ¼ mile S.E. of the right section. We fired 115 rounds at TX9—2 O.Ks, 18 Ys; 50 rounds at TX5 observed by Field Survey Section, very good results; also 15 rounds to register and calibrate No. 3 gun.

August 18th. We fired 170 rounds at NZ13—1 O.K. and three Ys. Later in the day we fired 70 rounds at the same target—9 Ys. TX11 received 100 rounds without observation.

August 19th. We fired 260 rounds at TX12—7 o.Ks and 28 Ys; also 280 rounds at TX11—4 O.Ks and 8 Ys.

The 20th August was quiet. On the 21st we fired 25 rounds at TX14 observed partly by aeroplane and partly by balloon, but the result was not satisfactory.

August 22nd was quiet, but on the 23rd we fired 60 rounds at TX12 with aeroplane and 50 rounds at an O.P. in Schoorbeck with Belgian double line observation; both these were good shoots. It was quiet again on the 24th.

On the 25th August we fired 260 rounds at TX12 with very good results. On the 26th we proceeded to the XVth Corps Rest Camp leaving the B.Q.M.S. and 10 men to look after the guns and and stores. Here we spent three days in perfect peace and returned to our position on the 31st.

On Sept. 1st we took part in a concentrated bombardment of point N.14.c.68.83. and fired 100 rounds at TX23 with Belgian observation, getting very good results.

There is nothing to report for the 2nd Sept. but on the 3rd we fired 225 rounds at TX15—7 O.Ks; also 80 rounds at TX20 with balloon observation getting excellent results.

Nothing happened on the 4th. On the 5th the right section was shelled from 3 p.m. to 5 p.m. with 200 rounds from 5·9 guns. No. 1 gun carriage was badly damaged and the position rendered unfit for further occupation. The next few days spent in moving the right section to A.5.d.o.3 about ¼ mile in front of No. 3 gun and our billets to A.11.a.3.8. just South of the Furnes—Pervyse road. The weather had become bad for observation. 2nd Lieuts. Allen and Burnie joined us about this time, and 2nd Lieut. W. A. Arch joined on the 13th Sept.

There is nothing to record for the remainder of the month except that on the 27th we fired 20 rounds on S.O.S. lines and 8 rounds registration on Chalet Farm, and on the 30th 85 rounds at NZ8 with Belgian observation. During October better weather brought improved visibility and there was a recrudescence of Artillery activity.

On Oct. 1st we did a nice shoot of 175 rounds at NZ8, the three active pits being destroyed.

On the 3rd we fired 100 at NZ8 again with Belgian observation. It will be noticed that we often fired at a battery after it might have been reasonably considered that its guns were knocked out. The chief reason for this was that the Germans were as hard put to it as we were to find suitable gun positions, and that we wanted to render the positions they had unfit for reoccupation.

Oct. 4th. We fired 22 rounds at an O.P. at N.20.d.o.7. with Field Survey observation—not very satisfactory.

Oct. 5th. Sixty small calibre shells fell near the telephone exchange which was hit.

Oct. 6th. We fired 60 rounds with F.S. at N.20.d.o.7 and very good results. Twenty rounds of 8″ or 5·9 fell round the right section and 40 small shells round the rear section—no harm was done.

Oct. 7th. We fired 136 rounds at TX8 with Belgian observation —good results. Thirty rounds of 5·9 failed to neutralize the right section.

Oct. 8th. We did a good shoot of 100 rounds with F.S. on TX1. Twenty 8″ fell in forward section.

Oct. 9th we fired 38 rounds at TX29 with Belgian observation and 60 rounds with F.S. at TX26. The Huns seemed to be quite cross with us this day. Between 1 p.m. and 4 p.m. both sections were shelled with 5·9s and 4·2s and our fire was frequently interrupted. Between 4 p.m. and 10 p.m. no less than 650 rounds of 8″ and 5·9″ were fired at both sections besides numerous shells of smaller calibre. About 80 cartridges were blown up and the position was badly cut up.

On Oct. 10th we fired 50 rounds at TX26 with Belgian observation, satisfactory. About 50 4·2s were fired at us and a few more cartridges were blown up.

On Oct. 11th we fired 132 rounds at TX26 with Belgian observation with very satisfactory results. Many rounds were reported "line" by both observers and two explosions and two fires were caused. The Belgians also observed 30 rounds for us on TX1 with happy results. Two hundred rounds from 5·9 guns were fired at the left section and No. 4 gun was put out of action owing to damaged platform and 200 cartridges were blown up. A few rounds of 4˙2s were fired at the right section.

Nothing worthy of note occurred during the next three days.

On the 15th Oct. 100 rounds were fired at the right section by 5˙9 guns. No. 1 gun was put out of action owing to damaged carriage and platform. Bad visibility prevented observations for the next six days. On the 18th I took over command of the group during the absence of the Colonel on 14 days leave. On the 19th 2nd Lieut. G. M. Pugh joined the battery, and 2nd Lieut. Allen joined about the same time. About a month previous to this Capt. Schoefield had left us to take over command of 69th Siege Battery. He was a most capable officer and most deservedly popular. It was with deepest regret that we heard later that he was killed on March 27th, 1918 during the German offensive. In his place Lieut. B. C. Thompson became acting Captain of the Battery. The officers of the Battery now were, myself, Capt. Thompson, and Lieuts. Shrive, Coursey, Burnie, Plumbridge, Allen, Arch and Pugh.

On Oct. 22nd we did a good shoot of 82 rounds with aeroplane on a dam in T.2.d.

On the 24th we fired 202 rounds on TX20 with aeroplane observation and good results.

On the 25th we fired 150 rounds at TX20 with F.S. satisfactory.

On the 26th we did a nice shoot of 382 rounds at TX20 with aeroplane, and also fired 8 rounds with Belgian observation at TZ8; this shoot was abandoned owing to failing visibility.

On the 27th we fired 104 rounds with aeroplane at TX20—2 O.Ks; also 433 rounds at TZ8—6 O.Ks, Nos. 1 and 2 pits reported destroyed on Oct. 28th we fired 508 rounds at TZ8 with excellent results and 41 rounds at TX22 with good results; both shoots were with aeroplane observation.

On Oct. 29th, 20 rounds were fired at TX22 with Belgian observation but the shoot had to be abandoned owing to bad light.

On the 30th we again tried to engage TX22 but after firing 14 rounds we had to stop again as our bursts could not be seen.

On the 31st we fired 120 rounds with aeroplane observation in TX22 getting satisfactory results.

The enemy had a few outposts in the flooded area of the Yser and it was decided that these should be raided by the Belgian infantry after bombardment. A large share of the bombardment fell on us during the next few days. A series of attacks by the Belgian infantry followed which were highly satisfactory.

On Nov. 1st we fired 300 rounds on Groote Hemme Ferme with Belgian observation. The shoot, was a good one and the fort was destroyed.

On No. 3rd we fired 300 rounds at Ferme Violette with Belgian observation, 25 of the rounds fell on the fort. We were shelled with 200 rounds from 10ᶜ/ᵐ guns.

On Nov. 4th we fired 250 rounds at Ferme aux Cochons; 20

rounds fell on the post which was destroyed. We also fired 110 rounds on Ferme " B" which was also destroyed. We were shelled with 160 rounds from 5·9 Hows. No. 1 gun was damaged.

On Nov. 5th we fired 280 rounds at Kilne Hemme Ferme which was destroyed.

We received a ration of 20 rounds from a 10°/ᵐ gun.

On the 6th Nov. we fired six rounds at TX9 and were shelled from 11 a.m. to 5 p.m. with 220 rounds of 5·9s. Ninety cartridges were destroyed. Photographs disclosed the fact that two concrete dug-outs still remained at Groote Hemme Ferme. We shelled those with 250 rounds on the 7th Nov. and destroyed them. No. 1 gun was put in action again on the same day.

On Nov. 8th we fired 48 rounds at TX9 with Belgian observation —results not satisfactory. We also fired 72 rounds on NZ59 with F.S. observation and 8 rounds neutralization on TX7. It may be noticed that our old friend TX7 had come to life again after a long period of repose. The position had evidently been reoccupied.

On Nov. 9th we fired 108 rounds with aeroplane on TX22, 159 rounds at UW7 with aeroplane, 19 rounds on NZ59 with F.S., and 14 rounds on UW7 with Belgian observation.

On Nov. 10th we fired the following neutralization shoots: TX7, 32 rounds, TX22 24 rounds, TX9 24 rounds, TX29 25 rounds, TX4 25 rounds, NZ1 15 rounds. We received several bursts of fire from small calibre shell.

The next two days were quiet. On the 15th we fired 100 rounds at TX9 and 32 rounds on TX7, both shoots with aeroplane observation and good results. We received 60 rounds of 10°/ᵐ shells.

There was a decrease in activity during the remainder of the month.

On the 15th 150 rounds of 5·9 How. were fired at us, and no harm done.

On the 18th 120 rounds were fired at us by a 5·9 gun with the usual results.

On the 20th we fired 100 rounds at NZ15 with aeroplane observation and 10 rounds with F.S. at the same target before the aeroplane shoot. About 50 rounds of 10°/ᵐ shell fell in our position.

On the 23rd we fired 200 rounds with aeroplane at the resucitated TX1 getting 5 O.Ks. About 60 rounds of 10°/ᵐ were fired at us.

On the 26th Nov. 72 rounds of 5·9" were fired at us.

On the 29th we fired 120 rounds at TX8 with Belgian observation as there were signs of fresh work at the position.

On the 30th we fired 58 rounds at TX1 with aeroplane observation and 42 rounds with Belgian observation. Results were good. We received about 100 10°/ᵐ shells.

Nothing more happened till Dec. 2nd when we emptied guns and left Belgium. I have given a lot of detail in this chapter with the risk of making the narrative tedious reading; but the artillery duel was such a remarkable one that I considered it deserved special attention. The following summary may be of interest.

Month.	No. of rounds fired at us.	No of rounds fired by us.	Hostile pits destroyed.
July	1770	2577	17
August	660	3218	13
September	225	534	2
October	1795	3075	10
November	905	2630	8
Totals ...	5355	12034	50

We also destroyed five enemy outposts and two O.Ps.

We had guns put out of action by hostile fire 15 times.

Our casualties were one killed and one wounded.

The estimate of hostile pits destroyed is a very conservative one deduced chiefly from photos. I should point out that we kept a big interval between our guns after the first few days and so made it very difficult for the enemy to completely neutralize us. There was ¼ mile between sections and about 200 yards between the guns of each section.

We were indeed sorry to leave many excellent friends amongst our Allies and they gave us a rousing farewell. A glance at the list of honours and awards in the Appendix will show how they appreciated our efforts. Many British awards were made to the Belgian officers and men who gave us such valuable assistance.

After pulling out on Dec. 2nd we proceeded via Wormhout to Angues (near St. Omer) where we were to put in a period of rest and training.

At 1 p.m. on Dec. 3rd the enemy fired some 5·9s at our vacated billets and got an O.K. on the officers' mess which wrecked it!

A confidential circular was issued by G.H.Q. under No. O.B. 751 in which " a few brief reports are given as typical instances of the devotion to duty displayed by the Royal Regiment of Artillery during the battles of 1917." Herein will be found a summary of our work from the 10th to the 24th July.

CHAPTER VI.

VENDELLES AND JEANCOURT.

We arrived at Arques on Dec. 3rd, 1917 where we were comfortably billetted and settled down to enjoy the novel sensations—rest and security. The fortnight which we spent here was occupied in drill, training and classes for specialists. During this period the battery was raised from four to six guns establishment; we took over two officers and about 80 other ranks from 183rd Siege Battery which was broken up; this added 2nd Lieuts. G. Bullock and E. Evans to our list of officers. 2nd Lieut. Burnie had left us just before coming here, as far as I can remember. The records do not always show the various dates on which officers joined and left the Battery and I have to trust my memory which is subject to correction. I should point out that it had now been decided that War Diaries were no longer to be kept by batteries, so that I have only private records to refer to from this time to the end of the war. On Dec. 19th the battery with four guns and a total strength of about 240 entrained at St. Omer, and preceeded to Peronne, which was reached on the 21st. The weather was bitterly cold and snow lay thick on the ground. We billetted here and made preparations to spend Christmas as comfortably as we could. The town had been completely and wantonly destroyed by the Huns before they were driven out of it by the French and British troops during the battle of the Somme. We were not destined to spend Christmas here, however, for on the 24th Dec. we were moved to some ruined huts near Cartigny, and there spent a really miserable Yule Tide.

We were now going into the line near the extreme right of the British front and had come under command of 76 Brigade, R.G.A. The R.G.A. had now been reorganised into permanent Brigades, and we were destined to remain in the 76th till the end of the war.

On Dec. 26th working parties proceeded to Jeancourt to prepare a position for two guns, which were mounted on the following day.

From Dec. 27th 1917 to Jan. 9th 1918, little was done beyond improving our position at Jeancourt, and there was very little fighting activity on our front. The weather continued to be very cold with much snow. Between January 10th and 14th we fired a few rounds at the villages of Bellicourt and Nauroy and at point G.14.a.90.25.

On Jan. 15th about 30 5·9s fell round our billets at Jeancourt with the result that Sergt. Green, Corpl. Ward and Gunner Marsh were wounded and evacuated. Sergt. Green was our N.C.O. i/c Signallers and was a serious loss to us. Quiet prevailed and we fired very few rounds till Jan. 25th when 185 rounds were fired with aeroplane at GD16 with very good results.

On the 28th we fired 35 rounds at GB39 with aeroplane, but the weather conditions were unfavourable and the shoot was stopped.

On the 29th we made attempt to engage GB39 and fired 76 rounds but the results were bad and the shoot was stopped.

On the 30th about 50 5·9s fell round the position without doing any harm. We started work on a new position behind a railway embankment near Vendelles for the other guns.

Nothing of note occurred till Feb. 3rd when six new 9·2" Hows. Mark II arrived at Peronne station for us. These weapons were a great improvement on the old 9·2s Mark I with which we had been equipped up to this time, and gave us an increase of range from 10,200 yards to 12,700 yards. For some days we were busy drawing our guns and stores and getting four of them up in the Vendelles position where Nos. 1, 2, 3 and 4 guns were mounted by the 10th Feb. We had done some work on a proposed position at Q.6.a. near Jeancourt but did not occupy this. On the 5th Feb. we did an aeroplane shoot of 200 rounds on G.B.41 with the two Mark I guns. The results were fair. 2nd Lieut. Gimblett joined us on Feb. 6th at Jeancourt.

On Feb. 13th we fired 70 rounds on G.22.c.52.95. and G.22.c.40. 80 in support of a raid by our cavalry who were holding the trenches.

On the 16th Feb. the four Vendelles guns were registered with F.S. observation: the results were very satisfactory and showed us that the Mark II was an accurate weapon. The forward section at Jeancourt fired 120 rounds at G.B. 26 with aeroplane, getting fair results.

On the 17th the rear (Vendelles) section fired 150 rounds at H.c.2. resulting in two O.Ks, three M.O.Ks; two pits were destroyed and one damaged and there were two large explosions. This was an encouraging bit of work with the new guns.

The 19th Corps took over our front from the Cavalry Corps about this time.

Conditions remained very quiet for a week, during which we improved our accommodation. On the 25th Feb. the rear section fired 50 rounds on the road from G.34.d.00.10 to G.34.d.46.46. The road was destroyed. A German offensive was evidently suspected to be in course of preparation and this shoot destroyed a section of road which the enemy would have to use if he made a big advance. We watched to see if he repaired the road; he did.

On the 26th the rear section fired 200 rounds at G.D.15 and 150 rounds at G.D.16 with aeroplane observation and good results. Nos. 5 and 6 Mark II guns were mounted at the forward position.

On the 28th a 4·2 gun shelled the rear position and Gunners Reid and Ennis were wounded. During the night we fired 35 rounds into Bellenglise.

On the 29th we fired 30 rounds on S.O.S. lines during a hostile raid.

On March 1st we fired a few rounds to neutralise three hostile batteries.

On March 2nd the forward section fired 16 rounds at G.D.16 and the Rear section was shelled with 100 5·9s.

On the 3rd the rear section took part in a half hours bombard- ment of enemy trenches and received 50 5·9s in retaliation.

On the 5th March the rear section engaged a battery which had been spotted behind a house in Bellengliss; 200 rounds were fired with excellent results to judge from the amount of ammunition that was exploded. Lieut. Shrive observed the shoot and photos taken before and after showed that the position was demolished. It was the best opportunity we had during the war of engaging a battery, with single line ground observation. The house behind which the guns were situated was identified easily from the O.P. and was a suitable ranging point.

The forward section fired 35 rounds with aeroplane at H.1.d. 50.15.

On the 6th the rear section fired 200 rounds at A.D.12 and 200 rounds at AD.11. The forward section fired 200 rounds at G.B.37. These were three good shoots with aeroplane observation.

On the 7th the rear section fired 10 rounds to register the road at G.35.a.1.9.

On the 8th the rear section fired 216 rounds at H.A.16, result: three pits destroyed, one damaged, and two explosions caused. Also

234 rounds at H.A.5, result, two pits destroyed, two damaged and two explosions caused. Not a bad day's work.

On the 9th the rear section fired 40 rounds at a suspected dump at G.35.d.05.90 causing an explosion.

On the 10th we fired 145 rounds in support of a raid.

On the 11th 30 rounds were fired at a suspected dump at C.34.b.9.1.

There were now many indications that the enemy intended to undertake a big offensive on our front. Amongst other things he built a number of bridges over the canal north of St. Quentin. These bridges gave us nice targets for aeroplane shoots and two were destroyed on the 12th, one at G.34.d.5.5. by the rear section, with 215 rounds, and one at G.22.d.8.5 by the forward section with 150 rounds. Two batteries were also engaged on the same day, 50 rounds being fired at GB5 and 70 rounds at AD23. On the 13th the rear section fired 135 rounds and the forward 65 rounds during the early hours on possible assembly areas.

On the 14th the rear section fired 140 rounds on assembly areas ; a few rounds were also fired before dawn into the village of Magny and the bridges at G.34.d.5.5. and G.22. d.8.5.

The 15th was another busy day. In the early morning the rear section fired 125 rounds on assembly areas ; then 133 rounds with aeroplane at G.B.21 destroying two pits and damaging two ; 220 rounds on the bridge at G.29.c.35.35. which was demolished, and during the night 50 rounds at areas where enemy tanks had assembled. The forward section fired 220 rounds at G.D.15 destroying two pits and damaging one.

On the 16th the rear section destroyed a bridge at G.34.b.8.5. with 135 rounds.

On the 17th only ten rounds were fired by the rear section at the road at H.31.c.00.65.

During the preceding three weeks the battery had fired three quarters of all the Artillery ammunition allotted to the Vth Army.

The next three days were quiet, the calm before the storm.

The enemy offensive was daily expected and batteries had been allotted special targets to engage in the event of attack. Four successive lines of defence had been marked out in rear, and battery positions selected to cover them, in the event of our being driven back. It was hoped that these positions would be held for some days so as to give time for reinforcements to arrive if necessary. It is now well known that our lightly manned trenches were overwhelmed in the first rush and that the rearward defences were never held continuously by the few infantry that survived to fall back.

On March 21st we were rudely awakened at 4.40 a.m. by a storm of shell falling in the positions and all round them. At the rear section the first salvo blew up the cartridges at No. 4 gun. It was evident that 4 or 5 batteries were firing at us and using a prouortion of gas shells. The road which ran close by the position also came in for a considerable amount of attention and was soon impassible for vehicles. All communications were cut from the outset and in spite of all the signallers could do, we had no communication with the Brigade or O.P. by telephone all day. I spoke to the forward section for about a minute at 11 a.m., but otherwise any massages sent or received during the day were transmitted by runners. There was an extremely thick fog which added to the confusion. The rear section guns were manned at once and opened fire on the S.O.S. lines. We continued to fire on these for some time, and then, in the absence of any orders from the Brigade we turned on to various targets with a view to holding up the enemy infantry. Fire had to be reduced to a slow rate as our ammunition was running short and there was no hope of getting it replenished owing to the heavy barrage on the roads. We were having a pretty thin time; our strength was being rapidly reduced by casualties, and it was extremely difficult to get any information regarding the situation. 2nd Lt. Gimblett and two men who were at the O.P. were all wounded and we did not hear of them again for ten days; they had got back to an ambulance, fortunately. So the long day wore on till 2.30 p.m. when we got our first message from the Brigade by runner, ordering us to pull out and retire to a position in W.6.a. which had been reconnoitred covering the nextinfantry defence line. We had very few rounds left at this time. The work of dismounting was commenced by a handful of hungry men; of course the cook-house was out of action, having been struck by a shell, and all the rations were impregnated with gas. During the afternoon the hostile fire decreased in volume and the fog lifted somewhat allowing hostile planes to fly low over us, dropping bombs and using their machine guns. They offered very tempting targets for our Lewis guns and rifles. I can swear that I knocked half the tail off a Hun scout with a rifle bullet. We only had enough men to dismount one gun at a time so it was a long job getting them all on wheels. During the afternoon our caterpillars arrived, having made an adventurous voyage across country. The guns were not dismounted and ready to move off till 2 a.m. on the 22nd when they started for the rear position in W.6.a. The mem were now thoroughly exhausted having been hard at work for 22 hours with only gas-impregnated air to live on. At 2 a.m. there were only 2 Officers and 19 men who were not wounded or overcome by gas.

I decided to move the personnel to Bernes, a village about two miles in rear, as the position was pitted with gas shell and we were without food and water. Accordingly after an hour's rest we fell in at 3 a.m. and marched to Bernes leaving a guard in the position. We could do no good by remaining in the position and we should certainly be in the enemy barrage which was sure to preceed his attack in the morning. As events proved we should all have been scuppered had we remained.

The guard joined us in Bernes not long after our arrival there with the news that the hostile infantry were in our position and had of course got all our stores and baggage. During the day Gunner Oliver was killed and 35 were wounded including Lieuts. Coursey and Gimblett. Everyone else was suffering from the effects of gas. The four guns with their carriages and beds were saved but were quite useless without their stores, beams and earth boxes. All office papers and personal kits had been left in the position and many articles could have been saved had we known the seriousness of the situation. The only definite information we had when we left the position was, that Le Verguir, just north of us, was in our hands, from which it was inferred that our second line of defence was holding out.

A reconnaissance carried out early on the 22nd proved that the enemy were well past our abandoned position and we got orders to march to Cartigny. On arrival there we were ordered to proceed to Peronne, but on the way we were picked up by some of our lorries and proceeded under orders to the appropriately named village of 'Misery, where we spent the night of the 22nd. During the day we had been in touch with Headquarters 19th Corps Heavy Artillery who had retired to Villers Carbonel. On arrival at Misery we were joned by the personnel of the forward section. Their story is as follows :—When the enemy's barrage fell at 4.40 a.m. on the 21st their attempts to get into action were delayed by the explosion of two of their cartridge dumps at the guns, and by the very heavy concentration of gas and high explosive. Their communications were all cut in the first few minutes, but they maintained touch with the brigade by runners till it retired. 2nd Lieut. J. L. Plumbridge was in command of the section and was admirably assisted by 2nd Lieut. E. Evans. They got the guns into action under great difficulties at 8.30 a.m. and engaged various targets with a view to embarrassing the enemy infantry. At about 11.30 the remainder of their cartridges were blown up and there was no prospect of getting any more owing to the intensity of the hostile fire. They awaited orders till 4.40 p.m. when Lieut. Plumbridge realised that the position was serious as Field Artillery and infantry were retiring past him. It was impossible to save the guns without caterpillars and lories so he destroyed them and moved his personnel to the position previously decided upon for occupation, in the event of retirement, in W.6.a. Here they managed to get their first meal of the day and unloaded some ammunition which arrived during the night. On the 22nd they received orders to retire to Athies and thence to Misery, where they joined the battery Headquarters at midnight 22nd, 23rd.

As already related the four guns of the rear section had moved off at 2 a.m. on 22nd to the W.6.a. position.

The caterpillar drivers under Lieut. A. A. H. Bilney, A.S.C. had a very rough time getting the guns out and behaved with great bravery and coolness. One driver was killed and one wounded before they got away. On arrival at W.6.A. they got orders to continue their retirement and they joined us at Misery at about 10 a.m. on the 23rd. Their journey had been carried out under very great difficulties as they were frequently shelled and bombed and the roads in places were well nigh impassible. Their performance was a remarkable one, and earned the M.C. for Lieut. Bilney, and the M.M. for Sergt. Woodcock and four A.S.C. drivers.

On the 23rd we proceeded from Misery to Proyart where the night was spent.

On the 24th we moved under orders to Marcelcave, and I was directed to form a reorganisation Brigade to re-equip and bring up to strength eight batteries which were in a similar plight to 91. This work was completed during the succeeding fortnight but does not belong to this story. It was possible to re-equip all batteries, except our own; the Mark II, 9·2 How. being quite a new weapon, for which no spare parts had arrived in France. This was a matter of the bitterest disappointment at a time when we could have been most useful, and we were compelled to wait for some weeks before it was possible to get the necessary spare parts and stores from England.

The 25th, 26th and 27th were spent in assisting the infantry to improve the defences round Marcelcave and in doing fatigue work at V. Army gun Park at La Flaque. On the 27th we moved to Rumigny and on the following day most of the personnel was distributed amongst Siege Batteries of the 19th Corps, which were in the line to relieve their sorely tried detachments. The men returned from the various batteries on April 2nd. The remainder of the month was very dull and was spent in drill and training. The enemy's effort on our front had spent itself and the line had been taken over by the Fourth Army in which we remained till the end of the War.

On April 3rd we moved from Rumigny to Pecquiny, on April 12th to Huppy, on the 27th to Villers sur Mareuil, where 2nd Lieut. Scott joined us on May 1st. We moved again on May 4th to Bourdon, and on the following day to Longpré just north of Amiens. During this time we were chiefly employed on ammunition fatigues at various dumps. We were now under the III Corps H.A. who had taken over from the XIX Corps H.A.

Since March 21st our chief object had been to obtain the necessary stores, etc. to enable us to go into action again. At last, on May 16th, we drew two platforms and on the 18th two guns and platforms and some other stores. On the 24th Nos. 1 and 2 guns were in action in a valley just east of Franvillers and west of Albert. The normal conditions of trench warfare prevailed. We fired from 20 to 50 rounds daily at various targets and did some nice shoots with balloon observation.

On June 6th Nos. 3 and 4 guns were mounted near Bresle, and became the forward section, 1 and 2 guns were known as the centre section. It now became the fashion to harry the enemy with Artillery concentrations which must have been most effective. These concentrations were usually fired during the night. A list of targets was sent out each day and at a given moment all batteries that could bear opened fire at a rapid rate for three minutes, at a particular target. We used to fire from 50 to 100 rounds at 8 or 10 targets in this manner during each 24 hours. These tactics continued up to our offensive on August 8th so the concentration shoots were in addition to any other shoots which I shall detail.

On June 14th we fired 50 rounds at a hostile battery XY6 with Field Survey observation and good results. A very regrettable accident occurred on this day. Capt. Thompson, Lieut. Allen and Sergt. Elton were examining a German anti-tank shell when it exploded severely wounding all three. Sergt. Elton died of his injuries four days later. He was an exceedingly gallant and capable No. 1. We could ill afford to lose him and the two officers who had rendered splendid services on many occasions. Lieut. Shrive became Capt. vice Capt. Thompson.

C

On the 15th June the forward section fired 168 rounds with aeroplane at XY6 getting 4 O.Ks during ranging.

On June 17th the forward section began an aeroplane shoot on XY33 but the shoot was stopped after 38 rounds by a hostile 8″ battery. The centre section engaged the offender with 72 rounds observed by F.S.; the opening salvo silenced it.

On the 18th the forward section fired 190 rounds at XY12; the aeroplane reported 4 O.Ks, 8 explosions and a fire.

On the 19th the forward section fired 50 rounds at FA4 by the datum and switch method.

On the 20th, forward section fired 50 rounds 'blind' at XY2.

On the 21st forward section received 100 8″ during the day fired at a slow rate. No harm was done. The Bosche was getting cross with the forward section for on the 23rd they were shelled practically all day with shells of various calibres. This sort of thing used to happen generally on days when aeroplanes could not operate. If a hostile battery was spotted firing by one of our planes, a wireless call brought immediate and stern retribution.

On the 25th forward section did a good shoot with aeroplane at XY37.

On June 27th a very successful shoot was done by forward section on F.A.13. 120 rounds were fired resulting in 2 O.Ks and many M.O.Ks. A similar shoot was done on the following day at F.A.7.

On June 30th we supported an attack by the Corps on our left by neutralising XY10, XY12, and XY32 with 95 rounds and forward section fired 120 rounds at XY3, getting some M.O.Ks.

On July 1st forward section did another very good shoot of 150 rounds at XY35.

By this time stores had been drawn for the remaining two guns. They were mounted near Contay and became the silent section. They were far to the rear, their rôle being to cover the retirement of the other sections in case of an enemy advance. Most excellent arrangements had been made to meet this contingency. So much so that we were beginning to wonder when we were going to act on the offensive. Be it remembered that at this time the tide of the German advance against the French was at its flood, and the daily communiqués were not calculated to cheer the British Army. We little knew how near we were to the turn of the tide.

On July 2nd, No. 3 gun of the forward section was dismounted and remounted in the centre of Bresle Wood about 300 yards behind No. 4. Thirty rounds were fired at XY10 during a hostile raid.

Early on the 4th July the Australian Corps on our right carried out its famous attack on Hamel; we neutralised KB21 during the attack and enemy counter attack, firing 130 rounds. Forward section fired 60 rounds with aeroplane at XY33; it was a nice shoot. All the aeroplane shoots were done by the forward section where the hardest work had to be done. The Centre section did most of the concentrations. To equalize the labour the sections relieved one another every fortnight so that there were always some men having a rest with the silent section.

On July 6th a good aeroplane shoot of 100 rounds was done at F.A.14.

On July 7th, 8th, 9th and 10th only the usual concentrations were done owing to bad weather. 2nd Lieut. Dunn joined us on the latter date. 2nd Lieuts. Anisley and Nightingale joined about the same time.

On the 11th forward section did a good shoot of 50 rounds with F.S. observation at XY61. Thirty rounds were fired in an area straffe in X.19.d.

On July 12th forward section fired 100 rounds at XY10 with aeroplane and 50 rounds at E.B.54 with visual observation, both were good shoots.

The number of rounds fired on the daily concentration shoots had now been increased; on the 13th forward and centre sections fired 120 rounds each, and about the same number were fired daily for some time.

On July 15th 50 rounds were fired at F.A.3 with balloon observation 2 O.Ks were recorded.

On the 16th an unsatisfactory shoot of 40 rounds was carried out on F.A.3. with aeroplane observation. Next day a good shoot of 100 rounds was done with aeroplane at F.A.13.

An experimental aeroplane shoot was carried out on the 18th. The forward section was ranged on XY9 in the usual way and then switched to XY33, XY2, XY7 and XY11 as prearranged, each of these targets being subjected to a short burst of fire. The experiment was quite successful, the M.P.I. being on the target in all cases except one. Other batteries tried this experiment but were not so successful, and it was not repeated.

On the 19th 108 rounds were fired by forward section with aeroplane at XY2. Next day the same target received 120 rounds, both shoots were satisfactory.

On the 22nd XY38 was engaged with 120 rounds and good results.

On the 23rd I took over command of 85th Brigade during the absence on 14 days leave of the O.C. and command of the Battery devolved upon Capt. Shrive.

On the 24th 40 rounds were fired to neutralize hostile batteries during a minor operation carried out by the 47th Division. Twenty rounds including 6 O.Ks were fired at the crater at X.13.d.6.5. with balloon observation.

On the 25th we supported a raid by the 58th Division by neutralising F.C.2. and another battery. A satisfactory shoot of 50 rounds was carried out with aeroplane at XY12.

On July 26th the two guns of the centre section were dismounted after dusk, and mounted on the 28th behind Bresle Wood, close to the forward section.

On the 30th a few rounds from a 5·9″ h.v. gun fell round the forward section. Next day some 4·2″s fell round the guns and 100 rounds were fired at F.A.8 with aeroplane.

August brought the pleasing symptoms of a coming offensive by us. The great French counter blow had started on July 18th and though it brought great cheer to the British Army no one dared hope that it was the beginning of the end.

On August 1st 30 rounds were fired with aeroplane at F.A.6 the results were not good owing to difficult observation.   During the night we supported two minor operations by the Vth Corps.   The weather had become unfavourable for aeroplane observation.

On August 3rd the enemy retired behind the Ancre on our front.

On August 4th the two guns of the silent section were dismounted and moved up to a position near Buire-sur-Ancre.   During the night 160 rounds were fired in support of an operation by the Australian Corps on our right.

On the 6th the Bresle guns were shelled by a 4·2″ gun.   140 rounds were fired at hostile batteries during the night.

August the 8th will be ever memorable as the day on which the great attack was opened by the IVth Army.   This caused " the break up of the scrum" and we found ourselves for the first time engaged in moving warfare.   The rapidity with which the " super heavies" kept up with the advance was a surprise to many and was made possible by the hard work and organization of the transport services. The battery was in touch with the enemy for the next three months except for a couple of very brief periods of a day or so.   This was because bridges had been blown up and congestion was tremendous on the roads.   A battery of 9·2 Hows. is not popular on a congested road during a dark night.   We kept up with the hunt from Albert to Le Cateau and beyond it and took part in the last big attack on November 4th.

On Aug. 8th at 4.20 a.m. our barrage opened and the infantry advanced.   We were in action throughout the day, neutralizing hostile guns.   The Buire section fired 380 rounds and the 4 guns at Bresle Wood 1000 rounds.

The 9th was moderately quiet as far as we were concerned till 5.30 p.m. when a successful attack was made on Morlaincourt during which the Buire section fired 280 rounds and the Bresle section 200 rounds.

On the 10th the advance continued and both sections fired many rounds on concentrations, " C.P." and "N.F." calls.

On the 11th the Buire section was in action all night and answered an S.O.S. call in the early morning.   They did a couple of good balloon shoots on hostile batteries.

Nos. 3 and 4 guns at Bresle began dismounting to move to Treux.

On the 12th the Buire section answered some N.F. calls and fired on concentrations.

On the 13th Nos. 3 and 4 guns were mounted in the grounds of Treux Chateau and their lines were registered.   The Buire section fired 50 rounds at a hostile battery; the aeroplane gave C.I. after 16 rounds.   They also fired on C.P. and concentrations.

On the 14th the Buire section did a good aeroplane shoot and neutralized four active batteries.   They came in for a mustard gas concentration during the night.   Nos. 1 and 2 guns moved from Bresle to Treux.

August 15th.   The Buire section did an excellent aeroplane shoot of 50 rounds and the Treux section fired 100 rounds on neutralization and concentrations.

From the 16th to 21st both sections were engaged in the usual harrassing fire and concentrations. The Treux section fired 50 rounds on the 17th at F.A.81 with good results; also 50 rounds at XY64 with aeroplane on the 21st. During this shoot we established a record of 5 O.Ks in consecutive rounds.

On the 22nd another big attack was carried out and all objectives gained; the Buire section fired 400 rounds and the Treux section 650 rounds.

On the 23rd 4.45 a.m. was "zero hour" for another attack. The Buire section fired 400 rounds and the Treux section 180 rounds. No. 4 gun was condemned owing to a crack in the muzzle. Nos. 1 and 2 guns advanced from Treux to Dernancourt.

On the 24th nthe Buire section fired 280 rounds in support of an attack and dismounted their two guns.

On the 25th the Buire guns moved to F.I.d.9. 4 near Becourt. This was a most interesting position in a valley which had been occupied by many hostile guns prior to our advance. There were the remains of many guns of all calibres and exploded ammunition was strewn around. There was an attack at 2.30 a.m. which the Dernancourt section supported with 100 rounds. The Becourt section fired on Maricourt.

Now that we were moving forward so rapidly it was impossible to keep all the six guns in action chiefly owing to the establishment of personnel not being sufficient. The system adopted roughly was to have one section in action, one section on wheels in rear and one section coming into action as close up as possible to our front line. In other words the three sections played leap-frog. In case of a check, we would have two or even all three sections in action.

During the advance the heavy artillery suffered from a shortage of caterpillars and transport generally, and many of the heavy siege guns had to be left behind, while their transport was used to help the batteries which were detailed to join in hunt. All the Mark II 9·2 Hows. took part in the fun but the 12″ and 9·2 Mark I Hows. were left behind.

On the 26th the infantry attacked at 4 a.m.; the Dernancourt section fired 60 rounds in support at extreme range and then dismounted. The Becourt section was employed in harrassing the enemy's communications.

On the 27th the Becourt guns did some good work on enemy roads and railways. The Treux guns were moved up to Becourt where they parked temporarily.

On the 28th the Becourt section continued their harrassing fire and two guns were moved up to Maricourt where they had a warm reception from the enemy's artillery. The position was too near the village cross-roads to be comfortable. In these days everything was sacrificed to speed in coming into action and getting rounds off. The enemy had to be kept on the run if possible and there was little time to select positions or to prepare them.

On the 29th the Becourt guns were out of range and the Maricourt section was busy on harrassing fire. This harrassing fire of the British guns caused great havoc on the roads which we found littered with shattered vehicles and the corpses of men and horses.

The 30th was a busy day. The Maricourt guns fired 130

rounds on the roads in C.15 and 16. The infantry attacked in the small hours and 32 rounds were fired in support on St. Pierre Vaast Wood. During the day 140 rounds were fired on various targets. Two guns were brought into action near Maurepas (or near where it had been before the battle of the Somme). Our advance was across the old battlefields of 1916 and nothing but desolation lay around from the commencement of the move forward.

On the 31st the Maricourt section fired 40 rounds on communications and the Maurepas guns fired 100 rounds in support of an infantry attack at 4.10 a.m.

It will be noticed that our allotment of ammunition at this period was not very large; this was solely due to the great difficulties of supply, but the moral effect on the enemy of a few 9·2 shells well behind his lines must have been considerable.

On Sept. 1st the Maurepas section fired 20 rounds harrassing fire during the night and supported an infantry advance at 5.30 a.m. The Maricourt guns were now out of range and were dismounted. This section was bombed during the night and Gunner Page was wounded.

On Sept. 2nd we lost 2nd Lieut. G. M. Pugh. He was carrying out a reconnaissance near Bouchavesnes when he was killed by a shell. This cast a gloom over us all; he had done some splendid work for us and was most popular with all ranks. His work as section commander on March 21st will never be forgotten by those who saw it; the detachment of No. 3 gun had been reduced to three men by casualties and Lieuts. Pugh and Allen with these three men fought the gun for the last hour that it was in action.

The Maurepas section fired 100 rounds with aeroplane at various strong points during the day and did some harrassing fire at a slow rate during the night. On Sept. 2nd the Maurepas guns fired 40 rounds into Manancourt during the early hours.

Sept. 4th was fairly quiet as far as we were concerned as the enemy was again out of range, and the state of the roads and bridges prevented us from following him, for the time being. The Maricourt section was again bombed during the night.

One of the bombs fell on some ruins close to where Mimi was spending the night. A wall fell on her and when the débris had been removed we found that all her upper works had been carried away, her body was riddled with splinters and it looked as if she would have to be abandoned. Her engine, however, was found to be intact so the wheelers and artificers got to work and in a few hours she was again serviceable but very far from being presentable. She was now entitled to six wound stripes, but we had no gold paint.

The 5th was again quiet but on the 6th the whole battery moved to Bouchavesnes and bivouaced. We did not come into action here, as the enemy was still out of range, and we had to wait while a bridge was being repaired before a further advance was possible. On the 7th we moved complete to Nurlu, remained there on the 8th, and on the 9th two guns were brought into action S.W. of Saulcourt. This shift was rendered most unpleasant by rain and hostile shelling.

On the 10th the two guns in action fired 70 rounds on harrassing and concentrations. On the 11th 20 rounds were fired. Bombardier Callcott was wounded by a splinter at Nurlu.

Nothing of note happened on the 12th, but on the following day a 50 round aeroplane shoot took place on a battery at X.26.c.9.1. which was fairly successful. The enemy artillery was particularly attentive during the night to the valley where the guns were in action, treating us to a considerable amount of gas. This was a frequent occurrence about this period. Another frequent nightly occurrence was the bringing down of enemy bombing planes. It was a wondrous sight to see a dozen or so searchlights concentrated on a Gotha; when this happened it was 2 to 1 against the Hun, who always dropped his bombs in a hurry and went for home as fast as he could; before he got there, however, he was generally overtaken by one of our fighting planes and then it was 10 to 1 against him. We saw a number of planes brought down in flames in this manner.

On Sept. 14th we mounted two more guns near Saulcourt, and many shells fell in our vicinity. A successful aeroplane shoot of 50 rounds was carried out on a battery at X.28.d.15.80. Our advance was now being checked by the enemy's desperate resistance at Ephey which he was holding as an advanced post to the Hindenburg Line.

The enemy artillery was fairly active on the 15th and we did an excellent shoot of 50 rds. with aeroplane at a battery at X.27.d.40.10.

On the 16th another good aeroplane shoot of 50 rounds was carried out on a battery at F.15.c.4.5. and hostile artillery was much less active. Gunner Newton was injured by the collapse of a dug-out and it was with very deep regret that we heard that he died of his injuries shortly after going to hospital.

On the 17th a very satisfactory shoot of the usual 50 rounds was done on battery located at F.2.a.8.5. The enemy put down a strong "counter preparation" during the night.

A big attack was undertaken on the 18th, zero hour was 5.20 a.m.; 750 rounds were fired in neutralising hostile batteries. Ephey, Pezieres and Ronsoy were captured.

On the 19th 150 rounds were expended on harrassing fire.

On the 20th Nos. 5 and 6 guns were moved forward to St. Emilie and the other guns at Saulcourt fired about 500 rounds. For the first time during the advance we had all six guns in action.

On the 21st zero hour was 5.40 a.m. Our ammunition supply was curtailed, but the Saulcourt guns fired 150 rounds and the St. Emile section got off a few rounds on C.P. and concentrations.

On the 22nd a few rounds were fired during the night on C.P. and concentrations and 50 rounds in support of an attack at 5.20 p.m. Nos. 3 and 4 guns at Saulcourt were dismounted.

On Sept. 22nd we had the misfortune to lose another most admirable officer in 2nd Lieut. E. Evans. He had been attached to the Brigade Headquarters for duty since the last week in May. A bomb fell on the Brigade Headquarters causing a number of casualties including very serious injuries to Lieut. Evans, to which he succumbed next day. He was an exceptionally gifted and capable officer who had endeared himself to us all. His work with the Jeancourt section on March 21st stamped him as an officer of outstanding merit.

On the 23rd there was nothing doing at Saulcourt and the St.

Emile section fired twice on S.O.S. and got off a few rounds on N.F. calls and concentrations.

The 24th was fairly quiet; the St. Emilie guns fired a few rounds on C.P. etc.

On the 25th the St. Emilie section did a 50 round aeroplane shoot. The hostile artillery was particularly active and we answered quite a number of C.P. calls. Nos. 3 and 4 guns were put in action in E.18.c; all six guns were now ready for the assault on the Hindenberg line.

The 26th was the first day of bombardment in preparation for the assault. The forward section at E.18.c. did a good aeroplane shoot of 50 rounds and the usual harrassing fire was carried out.

On the 27th Nos. 1 and 2 guns at Saulcourt supported an attack on our left, firing 90 rounds. The guns in E.18.c. did an unsatisfactory aeroplane shoot of 50 rounds and a satisfactory registration with balloon observation.

The 28th was quiet with the Saulcourt section, but the other guns did two good aeroplane shoots and the usual concentrations.

The 29th Sept. is another date which stands out in the annals of the war. The Hindenberg line was broken through by American, Australian and British troops. During the attack the Saulcourt section (Nos. 1 and 2 guns) fired 150 rounds and dismounted during the night. The St. Emile section (Nos. 5 and 6 guns) and the E.18.c. section (Nos. 3 and 4 guns) fired 250 rounds in neutralizing hostile batteries.

On Sept. 30th the news of the surrender of Bulgaria added considerably to the joy of life. The sections in action fired 120 rounds on C.P. and concentrations.

On Oct. 1st, Nos. 1 and 2 guns moved from Saulcourt and came into action in front of Ronnsoy; the St. Emilie section (5 and 6 guns) were dismounted. The other section at E.18.c. supported an attack at 6.5 a.m. firing 90 rounds.

On Oct. 3rd Nos. 1 and 2 guns fired 150 rounds in support of an attack by the Australian Corps at 6.5 a.m. Nos 3 and 4 guns answered some N.F. and G.F. calls.

On Oct. 4th another attack was launched at 6.10 a.m.; Nos. 1, 2, 3 and 4 guns fired 200 rounds on enemy batteries; Nos. 5 and 6 guns were mounted in front of Ronsoy near Nos 1 and 2.

On Oct 5th we supported another infantry attack in the early morning. Nos. 3 and 4 guns were moved up to Le Catelet.

On the 6th Nos. 1 and 2 guns were dismounted and moved up to park at Le Catelet on the following day.

On Oct. 8th another big attack was very successful, our cavalry came into action and advanced rapidly. Nos. 3 and 4 guns at Le Catelet supported by firing 100 rounds on hostile batteries.

On the 9th the battery complete, (less 3 and 4 guns) moved to and parked at Harbonniere Farm. The enemy was on the run now and there was no chance of our getting into action till he checked again. On this day I was ordered by the G.O.C. H.A. 13th Corps (which had relieved the 3rd Corps) to form a brigade, for fighting purposes only, composed of 19th Siege Battery (8″ Hows.), 91 Siege Battery (9·2 How.), and 312 Siege Battery (6″ Mark XIX guns). This latter battery was replaced in the Brigade a few days later by 143 Siege Battery (9·2″ Hows. Mark II). Thus constituted, Christians Brigade as it was officially designated, carried on till the end of the War. My orders were to keep these batteries of heavy Hows. up with the hunt. The Brigade staff had to be found from the batteries, and naturally my own battery had to provide the greater part of it. The only outside help we had was the loan of Lieut. N. Fee from 47th Brigade as signalling officer, and a most capable one he was. It was rather a problem to form a brigade staff and carry on under the circumstances and it was only the enthusiasm of the three batteries that made it possible to accomplish what we did. Had I my pick of all the Siege Batteries in France I don't believe I could have found three others that I should have been prouder to command. But this is not the history of Christian's Brigade.

The honour of commanding 91 Siege Battery now devolved upon Capt. Shrive.

The enemy's retirement did not stop till he reached a line running through Le Cateau which was directly in the line of our advance.

On Oct. 10th the Battery complete moved to Maretz and billetted. Here we found ourselves at last in a country that had not been utterly laid waste by war. Trees were growing and houses standing. The villages were intact, and most wonderful of all, they were occupied by French civilians, all very old or very young. Many stout hearts were swelled and many eyes were dimmed by the rapturous enthusiasm with which these poor people welcomed their deliverers. It was rather nice to sleep in houses again, the owners of which were only too glad to share their little all with us.

On Oct. 11th Nos. 1 and 2 guns were mounted at Reumont and a few rounds of harrassing fire were fired during the night. The hostile guns were very active and it was evident that the enemy meant to hold out on his new line as long as possible.

The 12th Oct. was a very bad day for us. We had fired a few rounds at active batteries and a few 8″ shells came back in return. Lieut. Ainsley, Sergt. Eales, Bombardier Newton, Gunner Graham and Gunner Mc W. McCullough took refuge in a cellar under a house, together with its inhabitants, nine French civilians. A shell hit the house and the cellar collapsed, the ruins of the house falling into it. Lieut. Nightingale was the first to discover the calamity and he, with Bombardier Bradshaw and Gunner Fletcher were conspicuous amongst many in the rescue work which was started at great personal risk before the shelling had ceased. The moans and cries of suffocating children were heartrending and desperate efforts were made to reach them, but in spite of all that could be done it was 7 hours before the last bodies were reached. All the civilians were killed except a little girl of 15, Marie Louise Lariche, who had a miraculous escape. The heroism of this child will live in the memories of all who witnessed it so long as they live. The bodies of her mother, brothers, sisters and grandparents were all removed before her eyes. She was pinned down by the debris only her head being free. She remained conscious all the time and gave most useful help to the rescue party in describing the structure of the cellar, and telling them where the other bodies lay. It was a scene full of many painful details which I do not care to recall. Lieut. Ainsley, Sergt. Eales, Bombardier Newton and Gunner Graham were all killed; Gunner Mc W. McCullough was taken out alive and apparently only badlyshaken, but he died from concussion next day. Thus only one survived out of fourteen who were buried by the shell. The work of rescue was exceedingly difficult as there was always the danger of the collapse of the small portion of the cellar which remained, and where Marie Louise was. The services of Lieut. Nightingale, Bombardier Bradshaw and Gunner Fletcher were suitably rewarded. The greatest regret was felt at the loss of Lieut. Ainslie and of the five N.C.O's and men who were all members of the battery from its formation. The deepest possible sympathy was felt for Gunner R. McCullough, on the loss of his brother. The whole incident depressed us horribly.

On Oct. 13th only a few rounds were fired on a battery in L.34.b. and there was scattered shelling round the guns.

On the 14th 60 rounds were fired with aeroplane on the brick-fields in Q.10.d.8.9. with good results. Nos. 5 and 6 guns were mounted in front of Maurois.

On the 15th the Reumont guns fired 50 rounds without observation on the brickfields in Q.10.d. and few rounds on concentrations.

On the 16th the Reumont section fired 50 rounds on the brick-fields in Q.10.d., 50 rounds unobserved on the Sugar factory in Le Cateau, and 50 rounds on concentrations.

On the 17th an attack was made at 5.20 a.m., the Reumont section fired 75 rounds on targets in R.1.c. and 20 rounds on Jacques Mill. The Maurois section fired 90 rounds on hostile batteries.

Another attack was launched on the 18th at 5.30 a.m. The Reumont section fired 50 rounds on targets in R.5.c. and 90 rounds on N.F. calls. The Maurois section fired 65 rounds to neutralize hostile guns.

The enemy was strongly posted round Le Cateau and to the north of it, and preparations had to be made for a deliberate operation by our infantry. The 19th was quiet, only 20 rounds being fired by the Reumont section.

On the 20th and 21st there was nothing doing. On the 22nd the Reumont guns fired 50 rounds blind on the quarry in L.10.c. and a similar number at the Farms in L.9.b. The Maurois section fired 20 rounds on N.F. calls.

On Oct. 23rd at 12.30 a.m. a very successful attack was launched. The Reumont section fired 50 rounds in support anl 20 launched. The Reumont section fired 50 rounds in support and 20 rounds on N.F. calls. Prior to this attack it was calculated that, if the infantry reached their final objective, an important railway junction S.E. of Maubeuge would be in range of 9·2 Mark II How. if they were mounted near our front line. It was decided to push up two 9·2s as rapidly as possible after the attack in order to destroy the junction. As Brigade Commander, I detailed 91st S.B. to carry out the task; all arrangements were made by Capt. Shrive and he personally took command of the section. The higher authorities subsequently called for a detailed report of the operation and the following was submitted by the battery.

On the 21st October 1918 it was desired to cut the German communications by destroying the railway junction 2000 yards east of Le Quesnoy. This task was entrusted to Christian's Brigade, who detailed 91st S.B. to carry it out. At this time the battery was in action a Maurois (left section) and Reumont (right section) with the centre section on wheels near the latter place. Our front line ran N. and S. just to the East of Le Cateau, but West of the village of Forest, whilst the nearest point from which the target could be engaged was on the N.E. side of the cross roads at La Balance. On the 23rd October the infantry attacked at 00.20 and a party of two officers and three gunners went from the battery up to Forest with orders to reconnoitre the roads and select a position for the guns. The roads were found to be passable as far as Forest though difficult in places, notably at Montay, where a railway bridge spanning the road had been blown up. Word was sent back to the column which had started at 07.00 and it proceeded to Forest where it arrived at about 10.00 and halted at the S.W. end of the village. Meanwhile the reconnaissance had been delayed—at first by bombing from low flying planes and then by the fact that the N.E. end of Croix had not been completely mopped up. Attempts to complete the reconnaissance both along the main road to La Balance and to the north of it were made by the officers in charge, but a continuous barrage of gun and howitzer fire at the cross roads and the vicinity made it impossible to reach this desired position by that route—though the party got near enough to the cross roads to see that the road was passable to that point, and that the cross roads themselves had not been blown up. One of the gunners of the party (Gunner Menote) was wounded during this part of the work and was taken back to a C.C.S. just established in Forest. An hour later, at about 15.00 the two officers and party succeeded in reaching the road La Balance—Boussies by the Croix—Boussies road and found the road passable though narrow and at one point in view of the enemy. The road was in addition, obstructed at the narrowest point by a land mine, which had not yet been removed or otherwise dealt with and which proved a serious difficulty, when bringing up the column later in the dark.

It was almost certain that there would be no opportunity for accurate resection of the position and accordingly one was chosen in two small fields which were marked on the map and this enabled the position to be plotted on the map with reasonable accuracy.

The shelling of the cross roads still continued, and it was therefore necessary to bring up the column by the Croix—Boussies road in spite of the mine, and to avoid observation it was decided to wait till dark. Meanwhile the line was laid out by prismatic compass and the pits marked out. The villages of Forest and Croix had been shelled intermittenty during the whole afternoon, and some bombs had also been dropped. One caterpillar had been knocked out and all the caterpillar drivers and Gunner Jones wounded by the shelling, and one limber gunner by a bomb, which fell close to the guns, but fortunately without damaging them. This rendered it impossible to take the gun up that night, as the A.S.C. Sergt. in charge of the caterpillars had to return in a lorry for more drivers and another caterpillar. (Telephonic communication had not yet been established). The distance and the state of the roads behind, which by this time were heavily congested by the advancing artillery of all calibres necessarily made this a long business.

The lorry column started for the position at about 17.00 hrs. and the lorries were all got safely past the mine, with the expenditure of a good deal of time. The task proved to be a very trying and anxious one for the drivers. Just as the column reached the position, the La Balance—Boussies road at that point was subjected to heavy and continuous harrassing fire from $105^{m/m}$ guns and Hows., and it was necessary more than once to clear the personnel to a flank. The men throughout behaved extremely well, only leaving their work when directly ordered by an officer to do so, and returning to work without the slightest hesitation. The gun stores (two lorries) R.E. platforms (two lorries) and baulks (two lorries) were all unloaded while another party of men dug the pits. While this was in progress 200 rounds of ammunition (10 lorries) arrived, and were unloaded and got away with only small splinter damage, though four of the drivers were wounded and some of the cartridges fired.

During this time the B.C. post, telephone exchange, and wireless post were established in a cellar about 300 yards to a flank, and the mens kitchen near the same place. When the lorries were all un-loaded and parked to a flank (the ammunition lorries had gone back) the men, who had had no food since breakfast, were broken off for a meal. (The ration lorry had become separated by the exigencies of the traffic and gone astray during the morning only rejoining just before the move from Forest.)

The shelling did not decrease and during the meal interval one man, Gunner Hockley, was killed and four wounded near the cook-house.

As there was no hope of the guns coming up that night and unnecessary casualties seemed certain to result from keeping the men at the position, it was decided to send them back to Forest for the remainder of the night. This was safely accomplished under heavy shell fire, a guard under an officer being left at the position. The shelling of the road and of Forest continued all night, accompanied by some bombing of the village, but it died away towards dawn, when the personnel returned to the position and the guns were brought up, mounted, and laid in the line of fire by prismatic compass and director. They were reported ready for action at 4 p.m.

The detachments stood by from dawn on the 25th to engage the target with aeroplane observation, but visibility was too bad and at 11.00 the order was received to fire 200 rounds without observation. These rounds were fired between 11.00 and 17.00 in batches of 20, searching and sweeping 100 yards. An aeroplane photo taken of the following day showed that the junction had been totally destroyed. Seven absolutely O.K's having been scored on the line, two actually at the point of junction. A subsequent visit by the B.C. confirmed the photograph in every particular and showed the rounds which scored the hits had been fired at the higher elevations. These results were obtained at a range of 12,800 yards (maximum range with pointed shell 13,200 yards), from an unresected position and with guns not recently calibrated (owing to the fact that during the advance there had been no opportunities of shooting with observation sufficiently good to give reliable results).

The officer in charge of the operations was awarded a bar to his M.C. and one N.C.O. received the M.M. The Brigade was complimented by the G.O.C. R.A. 4th Army and by the G.O.C. III Corps H.A.

On the 25th Nos. 1 and 2 guns at Reumont and Nos. 5 and 6 at Maurois were dismounted.

On the 26th an attack was made at 1 p.m., 50 rounds were fired on hostile batteries and 20 rounds on the railway junction. The enemy artillery was much quieter.

On the 27th and 28th we did no shooting, the opposing artillery was very active and interrupted work on a new position for 5 and 6 guns near Boussies.

On the 29th Nos. 5 and 6 guns were ready for action. The hostile guns were very active on the whole area round our guns where there was an amazing concentration of British Artillery. The Forest guns did some night harrassing fire.

On the 30th the enemy guns were still active. The Forest section carried out harrassing fire and were shelled throughout the night with H.V. guns, but no damage was done.

On the 31st the centre line of the Forest guns was altered from 30 Grid. to 80 Grid. Much rain and mud made it an unpleasant shift. The Boussies section fired 40 rounds on concentrations. Our area was sprinkled freely with shells of all natures.

On Nov. 1st the Boussies section fired 56 rounds on concentrations and the position was rendered very uncomfortable by hostile shelling. Capt. Shrive went sick with influenza and command of the battery fell to 2nd Lieut. Nightingale, who had been acting as my Adjutant. The Boussies guns fired a few rounds and were subjected to a shelling by a large number of pip-squeaks.

On Nov. 3rd the Forest section fired 50 rounds unobserved on an observation tower in Morval forest at S.17.c.1.5. The Boussies guns did no firing but were heavily shelled during the evening and night.

Nov. 4th witnessed another outstanding success for our Arms. The attack was delivered on a wide front and the enemy was routed. The battery opened fire at 5.45 a.m. and continued its programme till 9.35 a.m. During the remainder of the day only three N.F. calls were answered. Large numbers of prisoners passed to the rear. This was the last big attack of the 4th Army and from now onwards it was only a matter of following up the precipitate retreat of our enemies.

The state of the roads and bridges made it quite impossible for us to join in the advance. Our work was done. On the 7th Nov. the battery moved to Le Cateau. Christian's Brigade was dissolved and I resumed command of the battery. On the following day news was received that the German envoys were approaching. The next three days were spent in smartening ourselves up and getting ready to cheer, Nov. 11th brought the end.

As the staff of Christian's Brigade was almost entirely composed of members of the battery I feel justified in quoting the following order circulated by the G.O.C. Heavy Artillery XIII Corps dated 9th Nov. 1918.

"Consequent on the withdrawal into Corps Reserve, Christian's Brigade will cease to exist and the batteries composing it will revert to their proper brigades. They will remain in Corps Reserve. All personnel lent from other Brigades and Batteries to Christian's Brigade will return to their units.

Before the Brigade is broken up I wish to express my high appreciation of the way in which it was handled by Major W. F. Christian, D.S.O., R.G.A., and also of the excellent work of all ranks of the temporary Brigade Staff who assisted him."

(Signed) J. D. Sheerer,

Brigadier General,

Commanding Heavy Artillery, XIII Corps.

I cannot close without a word for the battery column, the officers of which were Lieuts. Lock and Richardson till the end of 1916, when they were relieved by Lieuts Bilney and Butler. Under these officers the column always displayed the greatest zeal and efficiency, and never failed us. They were in every sense part of the battery and both amongst officers and men the best spirit of comradeship existed. Our caterpillars did wonders and I am sure that no battery kept a higher percentage of lorries on the road.

APPENDIX I.

NOMINAL ROLL

No. 91 (Siege) Bty. R.G.A., proceeded B.E.F., France, from "White City," Bristol, 25th May, 1916.

B.S.M.

7797 Newton, J.

B.Q.M.S.

28355 Baker, C. A.

Sergeants.

24456 Baker, G.
 3490 Kennard, R.
35605 Kent, R.
 1952 Mescall, W.
20023 Odell, G. W.
20807 Taylor, W. A.

Corporals.

 6496 Clark, E. B. H.
30347 Clemans, A.
28645 Dixon, W. G.
29692 Green, R.
28647 Silvester, F. A.
12581 Wall, J. H.

Bombardiers.

28086 Bennett, E.
33584 Carroll, P.
28545 Chaffe, F. G.
32066 Hitchcock, L.
40779 Le Marchant, C.
38984 Riddick, A.
31418 Turnr, W. J.
31410 Underwood, S.

Acting Bombardiers.

43158 Eales, A.
34052 Goldsmith, L.
49464 James, R.
21243 Mountstephens, W.
19104 Smith, A.
31994 Stephens, F.
39035 Taylor, F.
22418 Willson, A. F.

Wr. Gunner.

67318 Spinks, T.

Gunners.

57541 Arnold, L.
51291 Atherington, E.
66931 Atkins, S. C.
 5800 Bailey, F.
53491 Bee, J.
 4846 Bickford, H.
 4774 Blackburn, J.
52366 Booth, A.
37222 Booth, L. W.
67323 Bowers, W.
64516 Boyce, A.
52553 Bowman, B.
66049 Brown, F.
60842 Brown, J.
67326 Bryan, F.
67284 Collcott, H.

65534 Carr, S.
61202 Chambers, R.
66833 Clark, F. C. C.
65991 Constable, W. A. C.
 4867 Cook, J. B.
64102 Cox, C.
67157 Crump, A.
64487 Davison, W.
65506 Douse, H. W.
28240 Duncan, J.
65483 Dunn, H. R.
60780 Fuller, C.
57615 Furlong, J.
65510 Gadd, J.
62410 Gascoyne, J.
43217 Geraghty, W.
65473 Gosling, B.
65555 Graham, H. M.
59901 Gray, F.
66058 Hampson, W.
66058 Hampson, W.
60826 Hampton, W.
57606 Harker, T.
64058 Harper, R. W.
48207 Harris, E.
65995 Holder, H.
 843 Holmes, G.
51332 Hopwood, J.
62414 Humble, A.
55807 Hunt, H. W.
60781 Hurran, S.
67582 Hutchinson, F.
 4875 Hutton, A.
64424 Jeffcock, C.
64414 Jeffcock, G. W.
 4811 Johnston, W.
64117 Jones, H.
60827 Laing, G.
65573 Leech, F.
42095 Lewis, E. J.
57573 Lock, W.
60893 Lucas, B.
64459 McCarthy, D.
62401 McCullough, R.
73687 McCullough, W.
66891 McMullen, A. F.
57530 Marsh, W.
57569 Marshall, J.
43027 Martin, M.
66132 Maslem, F. E.
63189 Matthews, E.
63059 Mamby, F. E.
65567 Mays, E.
66942 Menote, J. W.
60878 Milne, J.
48109 Morgan, A.
67154 Nacelle, T.
 1201 Neve, J.
66044 Newton, A.
62470 Noyce, R.
66804 Ogle, E.
64391 Oliver, G.
53599 Osborne, G.

Gunners—Continued.

67116 Palmer, A. C.	51507 Thompson, J.
64241 Partridge, E. B.	65906 Trimmer, J.
62454 Piggott, H.	52176 Troop, J.
67216 Postle, L.	62173 Turney, E.
51248 Rabone, A.	65538 Waddington, W. E.
64321 Raper, W. D.	62776 Walker, A.
66844 Reasbeck, H.	67709 White, A.
67051 Richardson, J.	62463 White, A. E.
64393 Ritchie, R. A.	67865 Whiting, C. F.
43161 Roach, M.	47779 Wildman, F.
4874 Ruddick, W.	66925 Wilkins, P.
62354 Rutherford, J.	64405 Woodall, G.
4873 Ryder, J.	47934 Wyatt, R.
64053 Shepherd, R.	60959 Young, G. A.
45874 Sheppard, H.	62348 Young, A. V.
1142 Sidery, J.	64377 Yates, W. H.
70434 Sills, R.	64338 Johnson, A.
64054 Smith, F.	67551 Bradshaw, B.
64502 Smith, F.	24964 S. Cpl. Lampard, F.
60897 Smyth, F.	13363 S. Cpl. Dalley, W. J.
65904 Strudwick, A.	57590 Gnr. Stone, J.
65977 Suddick, A. H.	
53525 Sutch, A.	<center>Attached.</center>
64471 Swallow, J.	
66967 Tagg, A.	1108 Armt. Sgt. Negus, D., A.O.C.

APPENDIX II.

Home Addresses of some members of the Battery.

Battery Sergeant Majors.

Fish, H. C.	58, Chesterfield Road, Copnor, Portsmouth.
McKay, S.	15, Radford Road, Plymouth.

Battery Quarter Master Sregeant.

Baker, G.	73, Cumberland Street, Portsea, Portsmouth.

Shoeing Smith.

Negus, D.	Carnbrea, Brittan Avenue, St. Albans.

Sergeants.

Murphy, A. G.	184, Hagden Lane, Watford, Herts.
Kent, H.	Oaksey, nr. Malmesbury, Wilts.
Stephens, F.	14, Brovet Street, Wellington, Somerset.
Young, P. S.	37, Kentmere Road, Plumstead.
Smith, A. H.	11, lyde Street, Canterbury.
Golightly, F.	2, Rose Avenue, Stanley S.O. Durham.
Sheppard, H.	51, Bedford Street, Buckland, Portsmouth.
Smith, A. J.	156, Northcote Road, Walthamstow, E. 17.
Stevens, P. H.	53, Cranborne, Road, Barking, Essex.

Corporals.

Robinson, T.	45, Bessemer Terrace, Low Spennyman, Co: Durham.
Wheaver, A. B.	39, Marston Road, Erdington, Birmingham.
Taylor, F.	155, Whitley Wood Road, nr. Reading, Berks.
Suddick, A. H.	5, Hadrian Street, Sunderland.
Thompson, S.	15, Ladypool Road, Sparkbrook, Birmingham.
James, R. W.	30, Holbeck Street, Burnley.
Sidery, J.	11, Evelyn Road, Walthamstow.
Richardson, J. H.	Woodside, Burton Joyce, Nottingham.
Barber, H.	Stoneleigh, Cheddleton, Leek, Staffs.
Matthews,	47, Stewart Road, Bournemouth.

Bombardiers.

Bambridge,	Roseville, Horse Shoe Corner, Wisbeach, Cams.
Barker, S. A. C.	37, Gibson Road, Hull.
Windsor, F. V.	Golden Hill, Stoke-on-Trent.

Names and addresses—*continued*.

Wilkins, P. H.	54,Lintaine Grove, West Kensington.
Morris, V. L.	8, St. Nicholas St., Scarborough.
Bishop, B. A.	Kingwood Common, Peppard, Henley-on-Thames.
Bradshaw, B.	76, Austen Road, Carcroft, Doncaster.
Callcott, H.	Valetta, Balfour Avenue, Hanwell, W. 7.
Harper, R. W.	12, Harefield Road, Crouch End, London, N. 8.
Mann, G.	Millward, Polstead, nr. Colchester.
Milne, J.	Bellmans Croft, Lonmary, Aberdeenshire.
Tant, G. H.	25, South Albert Road, Reigate.
Whittaker, J. W.	17, Rowan Road, Ardwick, Manchester.
Neve, J. R.	77, Bevington Street, Bermondsey.
Young, G. A.	40, Crescent Buildings, Martin Street, Crewe.
Harrison, F.	10, Suffield Road, Manor Place, Walworth, London.

Gunners.

Ansell, R.	9, Hastings Place, Lytham, Lancs.
Allen, J.	49, Francis Street, Cheadle, Cheshire.
Anderson, D.	27, Gibson Terrace, Edinburgh.
Austins, A.	91, Inkerman Street, Wolverhampton.
Alexander, H.	Rosslyn, Keneat Street, Inverness.
Alcock, H.	Burn Street, Carlow, Ireland.
Bannan, J.	18, Cicero Street, Moston, Manchester.
Bassage, J.	182, Queen Street, Beckenham, London.
Bassett, A.	71, Hornilow Road, nr. Burton-on-Trent.
Baylis, A. C.	Taxton, nr. Charlesborough, Oxon.
Beasmont, V.	Laurel Terrace, Stainland, Halifax.
Bee, J.	Beckingham, Doncaster.
Beechey, J.	2, Morstow Place, Evesham, Worcester.
Birrell, H.	41, North Street, Shrewsbury.
Blackburn, J.	20, Parker Street, Chorley, Lancs.
Bewman, A.	82, Frederick Street, Fenton, Staffs.
Booth, A.	5, Railway Terrace, Eastvale, Longton, Staffs.
Booth, L. W.	4,Ruscliffe Terrace, Bambergh Street, Meadows, Notts.
Brennen, J.	Coult Devenish, Athlone.
Buckland, A. W.	5, New Broughton Road, Melksham, Wilts.
Bull, J.	24, Lancroft Road, East Holly, London.
Bancroft, W.	26, Ashley Street, Birmingham.
Benson, T. P.	Ballybuttes, Queens Co. Ireland.
Burt, E. C.	80, Oxford Street, Pontyeyyimmer.
Carden E. B.	34, Shelley Cottages, Rest Hall, Denny Bottom, Tunbridge Wells, Kent.
Carr, S.	1, Turngell, Gateshead-on-Tyne.
Chambers, R.	Lake View, Bartra, Sligo.
Chadwick, H.	28, Molly Street, Blackburn.
Clarke, E. C.	5, Church Street, Hyde, Cheshire.
Clayden, W.	41, Gales Gardens, Bethnal Green, London.
Clifford, L.	183, Murchingson Road, Leyton.
Coles, F.	104, Berkley Street, Fosse Road, South Leicester.
Connelly, W.	15, Rodney Street, Cardiff.
Cook, A. F.	5, Coopers Terrace, East Street, Farnham.
Cooper, W. F.	19, Cheltenham Terrace, Newcastle-on-Tyne.
Cook, L. F.	45, Westbury Road, Bristol.
Cook, J. B.	45, Hounthersall Square, Clitheroe, Lancs.
Cooper, A. E.	Cromer Road, North Welsham, Norfolk.
Cave, T.	8, Derby Street, Ormskirk, Lancs.
Crowther, W. F.	14, Galena Road, Hammersmith, London.
Cockerhill, F. B.	21, Clark Street, Morcombe, Lancs.
Dickinson, G.	40, Milsent Street, Cardiff.
Dingwall, D.	Station House, Gogha, N.B.
Dangray, H.	136, Cassland Road, South Hackney,, London.
Douse, W. H.	7, Dolphin Place, Dover.
Dunn, H. R.	38, Abington Avenue, Northampton.
Dunkerley, J.	107, Oldham Road, Springhead, Lees, Oldham.
Drummond, R.	103, Mill Street, Rutherglen, N.B.
Devennie, J.	25, Maxwell Street, East Killbride.
Davey, J.	Hayes Cottage, Hurtsham, Bampton.
Dey, J.	Gardeners Cottage, Craigiebuckler, Aberdeen.
Evans, W. E.	75, Bramley, Pensonnett near Dudley.
Fletcher, J.	7, Melville Street, Chester le street, Co. Durham.
Fothergill, A. M.	3, Junction Lane, Orsett, Yorks.
Foley, J. J.	8, Harvest Street, Portsea, Portsmouth.
Farnell, A. A.	29, Earlsbury Gardens, Birchfields, Birmingham.
Fraser, J.	Burgis Hill, Radford Forest, N.B.

D

Names and addresses —*continued*.

Friend, W. S. M.	56, Coneybere Street, Highgate, Birmingham.
Gadd. J.	45, Cromwell Road, Tunbridge Wells.
Gray, F.	Crick, nr. Rugby.
Green, J. H.	23, Cranbrook Avenue, Cottingham Road, Hull.
Gibb, A.	Arden Gate House, Caldercruin, Lanark.
Gregory, W.	Lindis P.O., Hampshire.
Gibson, F.	3, Railway Cottages, Hart, W. Hartlepool.
Harker, F. J.	173, Reading Road, Henley-on-Thames.
Hampton, W. A.	Glebe Place, Kirkton, Burntisland, Fife.
Hargreaves, J.	Navigation Inn, Church.
Harris, E.	Highway House, 5, Pinock, Liscard, Cornwall.
Hibbard, G.	9, Millbrook Road, Brixton, London.
Hindle, G.	19, High Lane, Haslingdon.
Holder, B.	Brent Cottages, Greenford, Middlesex.
Homer, W. E.	High Street, Selsea.
Hopwood, J.	52, New Church Street, Radcliffe, Manchester.
Hornsby, R.	10, Ladypit Terrace, Whiteham.
Humble, A. A.	Court Cottages, Cudham, Sevenoaks, Kent.
Hurran, S. J.	3, Thrigby Road, Filby, Gt. Yarmouth.
Hutchinson, F.	79, Grosvenor Street, Leek, Staffs.
Hutchinson, B.	221, Pittercreiff Street, Dumferline, N.B.
Hulton, A. S.	7, Llangyridre Road, Beaufort, Mont.
Hughes, B. J.	10, Latham Street, Liverpool.
Hanson, C. H.	69, Plymouth Street, Manchester.
Healey, A. H.	Oakley, Chinnor, Wallingford, Oxon.
Tutchings, R. W.	38, Larefield Street, Queen's Park, London.
Hawthorn, J. R.	28, Gillats Road, Wood Street, Castleford, Yorks.
Hull, E.	Sutton Blacks Road, Hammersmith.
Holden, W. P.	7, Halfacre Road, Hanwell.
Hayes, B.	Millshure Farm, Croft, nr. Warrington.
Hodgkins, A. H.	31, Cramby Street, Saltney, Birmingham.
Hitchings, D. W.	29, Clara Road, Grangetown, Cardiff.
Hanson, E.	17, Audley Road, Manchester.
Jeffrey, H.	66, Kennetside, Reading.
Jones, R.	15, Park Street, Abersynon, S. Wales.
Jeffcott, G. W.	51, Westmacott Street, Newburn-on-Tyne.
Johnson, G.	Kemel Hill, Kirklinton, Carlisle.
Johnston, J.	170, Apparing Road, Glasgow.
Jackson, C. E.	Myrtle Villa, Blandford Street, Grimsby.
Kneale, J. R.	Ballamena Ballaugh, Isle-of-Man.
Knowles, C.	Thomas Street, Giggleswick, Yorks.
Kearney, D.	3, Evergreen Street, Cork.
Laing, G.	1, Roger Place, Coaltown, Fife.
Leighton, A.	Broomfield, Montrose.
Le Marchant, C.	Perseverance House, George Street, St. Peters, Port Guernsey.
Levy M,.	50, Bonner Road, Victoria Park, London, N.E.
Leason, J.	Poets Place, Hopwood Bank, Horsforth, Leeds.
Longhurst, F. B.	15, Baybiew Crescent, Swansea.
Lucas, B. H.	Mill Bank over Peaver, Knutsford, Cheshire.
Luxford, G. W.	6, Wallace Street, Warwick.
Lyle, W.	77, Bank Street, Loghgelly, Fife.
Ledgard, A.	19, Ilkeston Road, Marlpool Henor, Derby.
Logan, S.	169, Fontaine Bridge, Edinburgh.
Hawkins, S. A.	32, Cecil Road, Queen's Park, Northampton.
Hart, R. G.	54, Cobden Street, Coventry.
Hibbert, J.	273, Bolton Road, Stubbins, Ramsbottom, Lancs.
Hedge, F. A.	33, Hasel Street, Northampton.
Johnston, H.	26, Thurlaire Street, Leigh.
Marsh, W.	39, Wista Rond, Heydock, St. Helens.
Marshall, J. H.	43, Warnock Street, Leweno Mass. U.S.A.
Menote, J. W.	70, Frampton Park Road, S. Hackney.
McCrindell, E. E.	12, Arnside Road, Oxton, Cheshire.
McCullough, R.	49, Deckham Terrace, Gateshead.
McMullen, A. F.	233, Broadway, Cricklewood, London.
McMurray, R.	8, Cumberland Street, Edinburgh.
Metcalfe, H.	5, Westwood Road, Wilton, Birmingham.
McIntosh, G.	Dellas Villas, by Forres, N.B.
Morris, B.	31, Ashford Street, Farmwork, Bolton.
Murray, M.	16, Ebenny Street, Southwick, Sunderland.
Marchant, C.	Rose Cottage, Burley Street, Ragwood, Hants.
Morley, A. E.	16, Sandon Street, New Barford, Notts.
Medows, P.	Cold Fair Green, nr. Sakmundham, Suffolk.
Newton, A.	2, Laura Place, Plymouth.
Newton, W. A.	Sunninghill, Berks.

Names and addresses—*continued.*

Page, O. W. H.	Coventry Road, South Mardley, Birmingham.
Partridge, E. B.	22, New Road, Leigh-on-Sea, Essex.
Paxton, C.	70, Prince Charles Street, Middlesborough.
Percival, A.	Bowdon View Fare, Mere, nr. Knutsford, Cheshire.
Pett, R.	126, Hardybutts, Wigan.
Pickles, T. R.	Grassington, Skipton on Cravun, Yorks.
Pocock, G.	5, Milward Street, Manselton, Swansea.
Postle, L.	Gedling, Nottingham.
Price, W. G.	480, Belchers Lane, Small Heath, Birmingham.
Pringle, J.	24, Cobock Street, Carlisle.
Prime, W.	52, Otway Street, Garston, Liverpool.
Peters, E. A.	25, College Road, Grange, Essex.
Raper, W. D.	River View, Blackhall Mill, Hamsterley Coll, nr. Durham
Rixton, H. J.	Church Hill, Warmwell, Dorchester, Dorset.
Roach, M.	33, Buckyard Jump, Barnsley, Yorks.
Robbie, A.	36, Kirk Street, Peterhead, Aberdeenshire.
Roberts, H.	Newland Green, Egerton, Kent.
Ryder, J.	34, Forest Road, Leytonstone, London, E. 11.
Roddis, S.	136, Park Street, Masbro, Rotherham.
Scott, F. H.	14-244, Block, Gt. College Street, Kentish Town, London.
Scott, P.	1, West Street, Crawley, Sussex.
Shaw, A.	Carrgate, Bradford Road, Wakefield.
Shepphard, W. C.	Halfway Hotel, Cumbran, Mont.
Sissons, W. H.	26, Howard Street, Sutton in Ashfield, Notts.
Sills, A.	153, Grosvenor Road, Pimlico, London, S.W.
Smith, W. J.	1, Brunswick Terrace, Angle Road, Hammersmith.
Smith, E. A.	13, Carthey Villas, Hemmersmith.
Smith, C. W. W.	4, Lilian Street, Old Trafford, Manchester.
Smith, J. J.	84, Collingwood Road, Souirsea.
Smith, R. G.	Talbot House, Talbot Road, Luton, Beds.
Smith, W.	Plexholme, Duffield, nr. Derby.
Smith, F. J.	7, Goschen Street, Everton, Liverpool.
Smelley, C. H.	35, Spring Street, Derby.
Smallwood, A.	43, Newport Terrace, Brown Lees, Stoke-on-Trent.
Smelt, W. H.	22, Chester Street, Grasswell, Houghton le Spring.
Solly, E.	12, Pountney Road, London, S.W.
Stretton, J.	Ballymore, Dingle, Co. Kerry.
Sones, P. J.	170 St. Albans Road, Seven Kings.
Stokes, J.	No. 4 House, 15 Court, Gt. Barr Street, Birmingham.
Snell, H.	Heathside, Greyshott, Hindhead, Surrey.
Swallow, J.	1, Field Cottages, Belmont Road, Uxbridge.
Swann, J.	12, Oakley, Street, Northampton.
Spinks, T.	12, Netherwood Road, W. Kensington.
Sheppard, G.	3, Bonvista Place, Spital, Aberdeen.
Saunderson, J. K.	8, Wards Terrace, West Hartlepool.
Taylor, E.	86, Avenue Parade, Accrington.
Tagg, A.	71, Ouston Road, Carcroft, nr. Doncaster.
Taylor, R.	Yncleton, nr. Dorchester, Dorset.
Taylor, R. L.	14, Bishop Road, Bishopston, Bristol.
Tasker, W.	77, Ewart Street, Saltner Ferrn or Chester.
Taversham, A. E.	189, Lancaster Road, New Barnet, Herts.
Thatcher, G.	40, Dale Street, Rugby.
Thomas, J.	14, Horst Street, Crown Street, Liverpool.
Thomas, R. E.	13, Ashgrove, Bolton, Lancs.
Thomas, A. H.	Gately Park, Kingsland, Herefordshire.
Traish, A.	2, Trevor Road, Dundonald, Wimbledon.
Traver, R. V.	Beaminster, Dorset.
Unwin, J.	12, Cemetery Abenue, Sheffield.
Watts, A.	Thorncastle, Longstone, Stepaside, Amroth.
Waters, E. H.	Dunvards, Borden, nr. Sittingbourne, Kent.
Waddington, W.	88, Park Road, Wallsend-on-Tyne.
Watson, C.	13, Eardley Street, Long Road, Leeds.
Whittle, A.	11, A Winchester Terrace, Winchester Street, Sherwood, Notts.
Wildman, F.	Church End, Astwood, Newport Pagnell, Bucks.
Williams, H.	Cage Tandridge, New Oxted, Surrey.
Wilson, J.	Ferndale House, North Road, Bolton Colly, Co. Durham.
Wood, R. H.	2, Church Street, Althincham, Cheshire.
Woodall, G.	154, Prospect Road, Scarborough.

I should be pleased to receive the names and addresses of other N.C.Os. and men, who are not mentioned.

APPENDIX III.

Casualties.

Name	Casualty	Date / Place
Bdr. White, A.	Killed	Nov. 13th, 1916.
A.M. Allardyce	,,	,,
Cpl. Clemens	,,	Nov. 17th, 1916.
Gnr. Ritchie	,,	" "
,, Whiting	,,	,, ,,
Lt. E. B. Coursey	Wounded	,, ,,
Gnr. B. Neve	,,	Fov. 19th, 1916.
,, Gosling	,,	Arras, April, 1917.
,, Brown	Killed (gas)	,, ,,
B.S.M. Baker	Gassed	,, ,,
Q.S.M. Castle	,,	,, ,,
Sgt. Mescal	,,	,, ,,
Gnr. Walker	,,	,, ,,
,, McMullen	Wounded	,, ,,
,, Constable	,,	,, ,,
,, Palmer	,,	,, ,,
,, Ogle	Killed	Messines, April, 1917.
,, S. Jones	Shell shock	,, ,,
,, Maslen	Wounded	,, ,,
Q.M.S. Baker	,,	,, ,,
Gnr. Shklowsky	,,	,, ,,
Cpl. Robinson	,,	,, ,,
B.S.M. Fish	,,	,, ,,
Gnr. Whysche	,,	June, 1917.
,, Hodgkinson	,,	,, ,,
,, Sills	,,	,, ,,
Sgt. Carrol	Killed	Belgium, July, 1917.
Gnr. McMullan	Wounded	,, Sept., ,,
Sgt. Green	,,	Jeancourt, Feb., 1918.
Cpl. Ward	,,	,, ,,
Gnr. Ward	,,	,, ,,
,, Innis	,,	,, March 18th, 1918.
,, Oliver	Killed	,, ,, 21st, ,,
Sgt. Kent	Wounded	,, ,, ,, ,,
Bdr. Trimmer	,,	,, ,, ,, ,,
2/Lt. Gimblett	,,	,, ,, ,, ,,
Gnr. Sheppard	,,	,, ,, ,, ,,
,, Goldsmith	,,	,, ,, ,, ,,
Lt. E. B. Coursey, M.C.	,,	,, ,, ,, ,,
Gnr. L. Onyett	Gassed	,, ,, ,, ,,
,, J. H. White	,,	,, ,, ,, ,,
,, Whysche	,,	,, ,, ,, ,,
,, Travis	,,	,, ,, ,, ,,
,, R. Wyatt	,,	,, ,, ,, ,,
,, Davison	Wounded	,, ,, ,, ,,
,, Dimend	Gassed	,, ,, ,, ,,
Sgt. Dixon	,,	,, ,, ,, ,,
Gnr. Dixon	,,	,, ,, ,, ,,
Sgt. Bennett	,,	,, ,, ,, ,,
Gnr. Bowers	,,	,, ,, ,, ,,
Cpl. Taylor	,,	,, ,, ,, ,,
Gnr. Spinks	,,	,, ,, ,, ,,
,, F. Smith	Wounded	,, ,, ,, ,,
Bdr. S. Parker	Gassed	,, ,, ,, ,,
Gnr. A. White	,,	,, ,, ,, ,,
,, Osborne	Wounded	,, ,, ,, ,,
,, Mawby	Gassed	,, ,, ,, ,,
,, Gascoyne	Wounded	,, ,, ,, ,,
,, Jeffcott, G.	Gassed	,, ,, ,, ,,
,, Jeffcott, G. W.	,,	,, ,, ,, ,,
,, Cook, J. B.	,,	,, ,, ,, ,,
,, Cox, C.	Wounded	,, ,, ,, ,,
,, Weston	,,	,, ,, ,, ,,
,, Roberts	,,	,, ,, ,, ,,
Sgt. A. Smith	Gassed	,, ,, ,, ,,
Bdr. W. Royce	,,	,, ,, ,, ,,
Gnr. Bryan	,,	,, ,, ,, ,,
Bdr. Bishop	,,	,, ,, ,, ,,
Gnr. Hayes	,,	,, ,, ,, ,,
,, Jarret	,,	,, ,, ,, ,,
Capt. B. C. Thompson	Accidentally wounded	Contay, June, 1218.
2/Lt. B. Allen	,,	,, ,,
Sgt. Elton	Accidentally killed	,, ,,
Gnr. Webdale	Killed	,, ,,
,, V. Beaumont	Wounded	Bresle, ,,
,, Rixton	,,	,, ,,
Sgt. Webster	Gassed	,, ,,
Gnr. Leighton	,,	Lavieville, July, 1918.
,, Turner	,,	Buire, Aug. 10th, ,,
Bdr. Duncan	,,	Treuk, ,, 18th ,,
,, Harper	D.A.H. from gas	,, Sept. 3rd
2/Lt. M. M. Pugh	Killed	Bouchavesnes, Sept., 1918.

Gnr. Benson ...	...	...	...	Wounded	...	...	...	Buire,	,,	,,
,, Page	...	...	...	,,	...	...	...	Maricourt,	,,	,,
,, Alexander	...	...	...	Gassed ...	...	...	...	Saulcourt,	,,	20th.
,, Weir	...	...	...	,, ...	...	...	...	,,	,,	,,
,, Burt	...	...	...	,, ...	...	...	...	,,	,,	,,
Bdr. Callcott ...	...	...	...	Wounded	...	...	...	Nurlu,	,,	,,
2/Lt. E. Evans	...	...	...	Killed ...	...	...	...	Villers Faucon, Sept., 1918.		
Gnr. Baylis ...	...	...	...	Wounded	...	...	...			
,, Peters ...	...	...	...	,,	...	...	...	St. Emilie, Sept. 25th, ,,		
,, S. Carr ...	...	...	...	Gassed ...	...	...	...	Reumont, Oct., 1918.		
Lt. A. R. Ainsley	...	...	...	Killed ...	...	...	...	,, Oct. 10th, 1918.		
Sgt. Eales ...	...	...	...	,,	...	...	...	,,	,,	,,
A/Bdr. Newton	...	...	...	,,	...	...	...	,,	,,	,,
Gnr. Graham ...	...	...	...	,,	...	...	...	,,	,,	,,
,, McCullough, W.	...	...	...	,,	...	...	...	,,	,,	,,
,, W. Menote	...	...	...	Wounded	...	...	...	Boussies, Oct. 23rd, 1918.		
,, Gregory	...	...	...	,,	...	...	...	,,	,,	,,
,, Buckland	...	...	...	,,	...	...	...	,,	,,	,,
,, E. Solly ...	...	...	...	,,	...	...	...	,,	,,	,,
,, Foley ...	...	...	...	,,	...	...	...	,,	,,	,,
,, Jones, R.	...	...	...	,,	...	...	...	,,	,,	,,
,, Dongray, H.	...	...	...	{ Wounded and died of } influenza				,,	,,	,,
,, Hockley, F. ...	...	...	...	Killed ...	...	...	...	,,	,,	,,
,, Jeffcott, G. H. ...	...	...	...	Wounded	...	...	...	,, ,, 24th, 1918.		
Sgt. Bennett ...	...	...	...	Died of influenza	...	...	...	,, Nov., 1918.		
Gnr. Atherington	...	...	...	,,	,,	...	...	,,	,,	,,

TOTAL.

8 officers and 16 O.Rs.	...	...	...	Killed.
5 officers and 81 O.Rs.	...	...	...	Wounded and gassed.
3 O.Rs. died of influenza.				Total casualties, 108.

APPENDIX IV.

List of Honours and Awards.

NAME.				HONOUR OR AWARD.
Major W. F. Christian ...	...	...		D.S.O., mentioned in despatches (three times), Chevalier of the Order of Leopold, Croix de Guerre (Belgian).
Capt. R. Shrive ...	...	...	...	M.C. and Bar, Chevalier of the Order of Couronne, Croix de Guerre (Belgian).
Lieut. E. P. Coursey	...	...	...	M.C,, Chevalier of the Order of Couronne, Croix de Guerre (Belgian).
Capt. B. C. Thompson ...	...	...		M.C.
Lieut. J. K. Plumbridge	...	...		M.C.
Lieut. R. D. Nightingale	...	...		M.C.
Sergt. R. Kent ...	...	...		D.C.M., Order of Leopold II, Croix de Guerre (Belgian).
Sergt. R. Green ...	...	...		Order of Leopold II, Croix de Guerre (Belgian).
Bombr. A. H. Suddick ...	...	...		Croix de Guerre ⎫
Gunner W. Lock ...	...	...		Croix de Guerre ⎬ Belgian.
Bombr. Stott ...	...	...		Croix de Guerre ⎪
Gunner A. Hampton	...	...		Croix de Guerre ⎭
A.M. Routledge ...	...	...		Croix de Guerre (French).
Sergt. F. Stephens	...	...		M.M.
Gunner Harrison...	...	...		M.M.
Bombr. B. Bradshaw	...	...		M.M.
Gunner J. Fletcher	...	...		M.M.
Bombr. E. Matthews	...	...		M.M.
S. Sergt. E. Negus	...	...		M.S.M.
Corpl. A. B. Wheaver	...	...		M.S.M.
Sergt. Carrol ...	...	...		⎫
Sergt. Green ...	...	...		⎬ Certificates of Gallantry from Corps Commander.
Gunner Lock ...	...	...		⎭

APPENDIX V.

W.Os., N.C.Os., and Men with 91st Siege Battery, R.G.A., on November, 11th, 1918.

Name	Rank	Number
Ason, E.	Gunner	177059
Alcock, H.	,,	182717
Allison, J.	,,	152305
Alsop, G.	,,	188717
Anderson, D.	,.	82078
Ansell, R.	Ftr. Gnr.	678719
Arnett, G.	Gunner	144609
Ashpole, G. H.	,,	51291
Atherington, E.	,,	94232
Austins, A.	,,	154621
Baker, A. E.	,,	38899
Baker, W.	,,	182723
Ballantyne, J.	,,	203762
Bancroft, W.	,,	85671
Bannan, J.	,,	81298
Barber, H.	A/Sgt.	213804
Bastin, J.	Gunner	134494
Bassage, J.	,,	61545
Bassett, A.	,,	145977
Beavis, H.	,,	143600
Beaumont, V.	,,	129566
Beechey, J.	,,	53491
Bee, J.	,,	348651
Bell, A.	,,	209509
Bennett, E.	Sgt.	28086
Benson, T.	Gunner	57817
Betties, A.	,,	38480
Bibby, T.	,,	123897
Birrell, H.	,,	141514
Bishop(J.	,,	205101
Bishop, B. A.	L/Bdr.	91609
Blackburn, J.	Gunner	279774
Blunt, B.	,,	139838
Booth, A.	,,	52366
Bradshaw, B.	F/Bdr.	67551
Bradshaw, G. R.	Gunner	197333
Brennan, J.	,,	3169
Brockwell, P. V.	,.	196779
Brundell, C. F.	,,	130314
Brompton, A.	,,	151552
Bushnell, T.	,,	49728
Bull, J.	,,	87969
Carr, S.	,,	65534
Carden, A. E. J.	,,	56323
Cave, T.	,.	93003
Chadwick, H.	,,	334642
Chambers, R.	,,	61202
Clarke, E.	,,	92090
Clifford, L.	,,	316305
Coles,	,,	104198
Cockerill, F. B.	,,	218383
Cooper, W. F.	L/Bdr.	83994
Cook, L. F.	Gunner	116430
Cooper, A. E.	,,	93709
Cowler, F. W.	Fitter	42116
Croftes, F. W.	Sgt.	30502
Crump, A. E.	Gunner	67157
Cutting, A.	,,	104759
Cuss, R.	,,	78676
Davey, J.	,,	170074
Dennis, W. R.	,,	186201
Devennie, J.	,,	190872
Dey, J.	.,	207052
Dickenson, G.	,,	92850
Dingwall, D.	,,	128991
Douse, H. W.	,,	65306
Drummond, R.	,,	190784
Duncan, J.	,,	28240
Dunn, H. R.	,,	65483
Dunkerley, J.	,,	344545
Evans, W. E.	,,	177285
Farrell, A. A.	,,	121003
Fletcher, J.	,,	155041
Foley, J. J.	.,	196700
Fothergill, A. M.	.,	104473
Fraser, J.	,,	204034
Friend, W.	,	194636
Freakley, W. L.	Gunner	209335
George, A.	,,	306306
Gilpin, W.	B.S.M.	13992
Gray, F.	Gunner	59901
Green, J. H.	,,	166917
Gregory, W.	Sgt.	204284
Hampton, W. T.	Gunner	60126
Harker, T. J.	,,	57606
Harper, R. W.	A/Bdr.	64058
Harris, E.	Gunner	48207
Harrison, F. J.	,'	26035
Hart, R. G.	,,	190770
Hawkins, S. A. V.	,,	179276
Hayes, E.	,,	67915
Healey, E.	,,	190056
Headge, F. A.	,,	209603
Hibbard, G.	,,	132099
Higginbottom, J.	.,	92046
Hogge, E.	,,	174413
Holder, B.	,,	65995
Hopwood, J.	,,	51332
Hughes, P.	,,	139223
Humble, A. A.	,,	62414
Hurren, S. J.	,,	60781
Hutchinson, J.	,,	306285
Hutchinson, F.	,,	65782
Hutton, A. S.	,,	279875
Hutchings, R.	,,	139952
Jackson, J. E.	,,	176896
James, R. W.	Bdr.	49464
Johnston, J,	Gunner	182600
Johnson, J.	,,	174437
Johnson, H.	,,	218293
Kent, H.	Sgt.	35605
Kneale, J. R.	Gunner	92479
Laing, G.	,,	60827
Le Marchant, C.	,,	40779
Lowdon, E.	,,	104505
Lucas, B.	,,	60893
Luxford	,,	116159
Lyle, W.	,,	306487
Mann, C.	,,	50190
Marsh, W.	,,	57590
Marshall, J. H.	F/Gunner	187135
Marchant, C.	Gunner	144935
Matthews, E.	A/Bdr.	63189
McIntosh, G.	Gunner	204040
McKay, S.	B.S.M.	22583
McCullough, R.	Gunner	62401
Messall, W.	B.Q.M.S.	1952
Meadows. P.	Gunner	17974
Millard, C.	,,	75238
Milne, J.	,,	60878
Mills, A.	,,	217193
Morris, N. L.	L/Bdr.	338616
Morgan, W.	Gunner	199360
Murray. W.	,,	189284
Murray, R. M.	,,	144885
Nacelle, S. J.	,,	67154
Neve, J. R.	A/L/Bdr.	276201
Northcott, W. J.	Gunner	218890
O'Keefe, M.	,,	27585
Onyett, L.	,,	150957
Partridge, E. J.	,,	64241
Parry, M.	,,	123845
Patrick, W. J.	,,	141117
Peet, R.	,,	161159
Percival, A.	,,	86502
Pett, S. G.	Sgt.	25163
Pickles, T. R.	Gunner	104355
Pilbean, R. H.	,,	210045
Pocock, G.	,,	92840
Postle, L.	,,	67216
Price, W. S.	,,	135549
Pringle,	,,	180695
Prime, W.	,,	102915
Pritchard, E. C.	,,	181055

Name	Rank	Number
Prosser, P.	Gunner	135859
Rand, H.	,,	154073
Raper, W. D.	,,	64331
Read, G. C.	Sig.	178160
Richardson, J. H.	A/Bdr.	67051
Ritton, H. J.	Gunner	91271
Roach, M.	,,	43161
Robinson, T.	A/Cpl.	54858
Roddis, S.	Gunner	89246
Rutherford, J.	,,	62354
Ryder, J.	,,	279773
Scutt, F.	,,	73834
Seaman, A.	,	189994
Shaw, A.	,,	88927
Sheppard, W. C.	,,	123893
Sheppard, H.	Sgt.	45874
Sheppard, J.	,,	203946
Sidery, J.	A/Cpl.	276142
Sills, A. J.	Gunner	70434
Sissons, W. H.	,,	104306
Smallwood, A.	,,	112696
Smedley, C. H.	,,	142793
Smelt, H. W.	,,	175942
Smith, A.	Cpl.	19104
Smith, F. J.	Gunner	60897
Smith, J. J.	,,	135313
Smith, A. H.	Sgt.	26264
Smith, W. J.	Gunner	119976
Smith, E. A.	,,	108345
Snell, H. P.	,,	60685
Sones, P. J.	,,	90296
Smith, W.	,,	167221
Spinks, T. W.	W/Gnr.	67318
Stevens, P. H.	Cpl.	340595
Stevens, F.	Cpl.	31994
Stokes, J. T.	Gunner	183391
Stretton, J. J.	,,	2831
Suddick, A. H.	Cpl.	65977
Swallow, J.	Gunner	64471
Swan, W. J.	,,	59217
Tagg, A.	,,	66967
Tant, G. H.	,,	101175
Tasker, W.	,,	196905
Taylor, R. L.	,,	37334
Taylor, R.	,,	58117
Taylor, E.	,,	334779
Tay'or, F.	Sgt.	89085
Teversham, A.	Gunner	44900
Thatcher, V. G.	,,	190178
Thomas, E.	,,	174225
Thomas, J.	,,	112937
Thompson, S.	Cpl.	38967
Traish, A.	Gunner	147559
Travers, R. V.	,,	110194
Unwin, J.	,,	122579
Wheaver, A. B.	Bdr.	78705
Whittle, A.	Gunder	88929
Whittaker, J. W.	A/Bdr.	112674
Wildman, F.	Gunner	47779
Wilkins, P. H.	A/Bdr.	66925
Williams, H.	Gunner	105152
Wilson, J.	,,	80601
Windsor, F. V.	Bdr.	71260
Wood, R. H.	Gunner	97660
Woodall, G. W.	,,	64405
Wooding, A.	,,	376586
Young, A. V. G. A.	,,	60959
Young, P.	Sgt.	19420

POSITIONS OCCUPIED

during

BAPAUME

Battery F

POSITIONS OCCUPIED BY 91ST SIEGE BATTERY, R.G.A.

During the Advance of 1918.

CAMBRAI

ST SIEGE BATTERY, R.G.A.

vance of 1918.

Spread 1

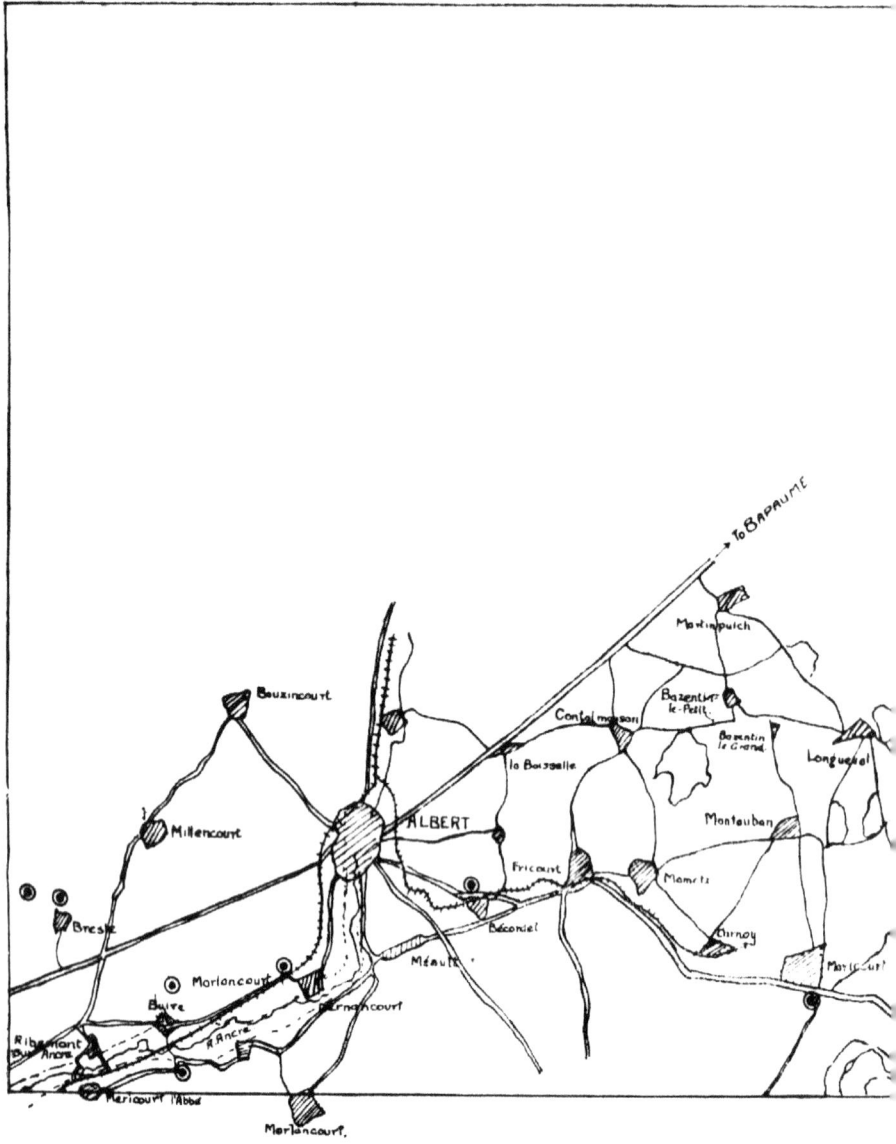

POSITIONS OCCUPIED BY

during the

BAPAUMÈ

Morval

Ginchy

illemont   Comble

Rancou

Nurlu

Hardecourt
aux Bois

le Forest

Moislarns

Lieramont

Maure pos

Bouchavesnes

Aizecourt
le-Bas

Curlu

Cléry

Allaine

Aizecourt le Haut

Templeux
la-Fosse

Villers-laricon

Longavesnes

Fins

Ennifis

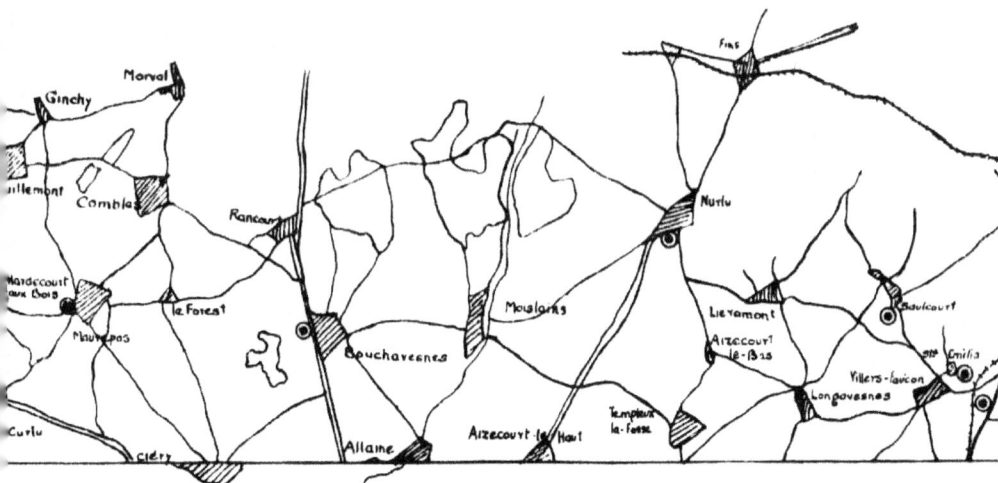

Battery Position

CAMBRAI

BEAUVOIS

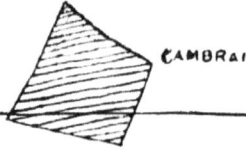

91ST SIEGE BATTERY, R.G.A.

Advance of 1918.

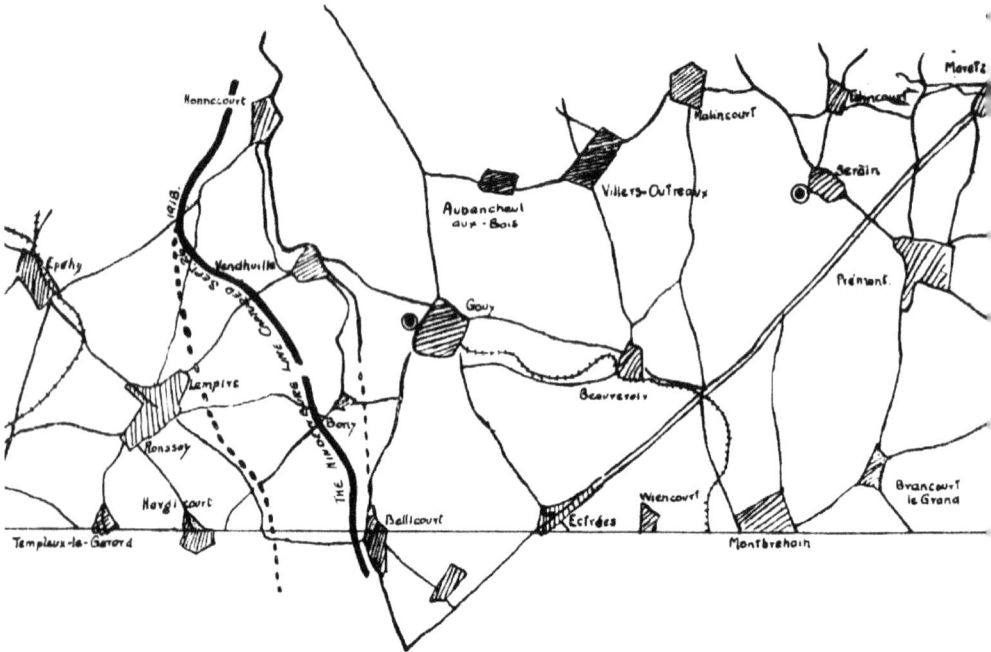

marked ⊙

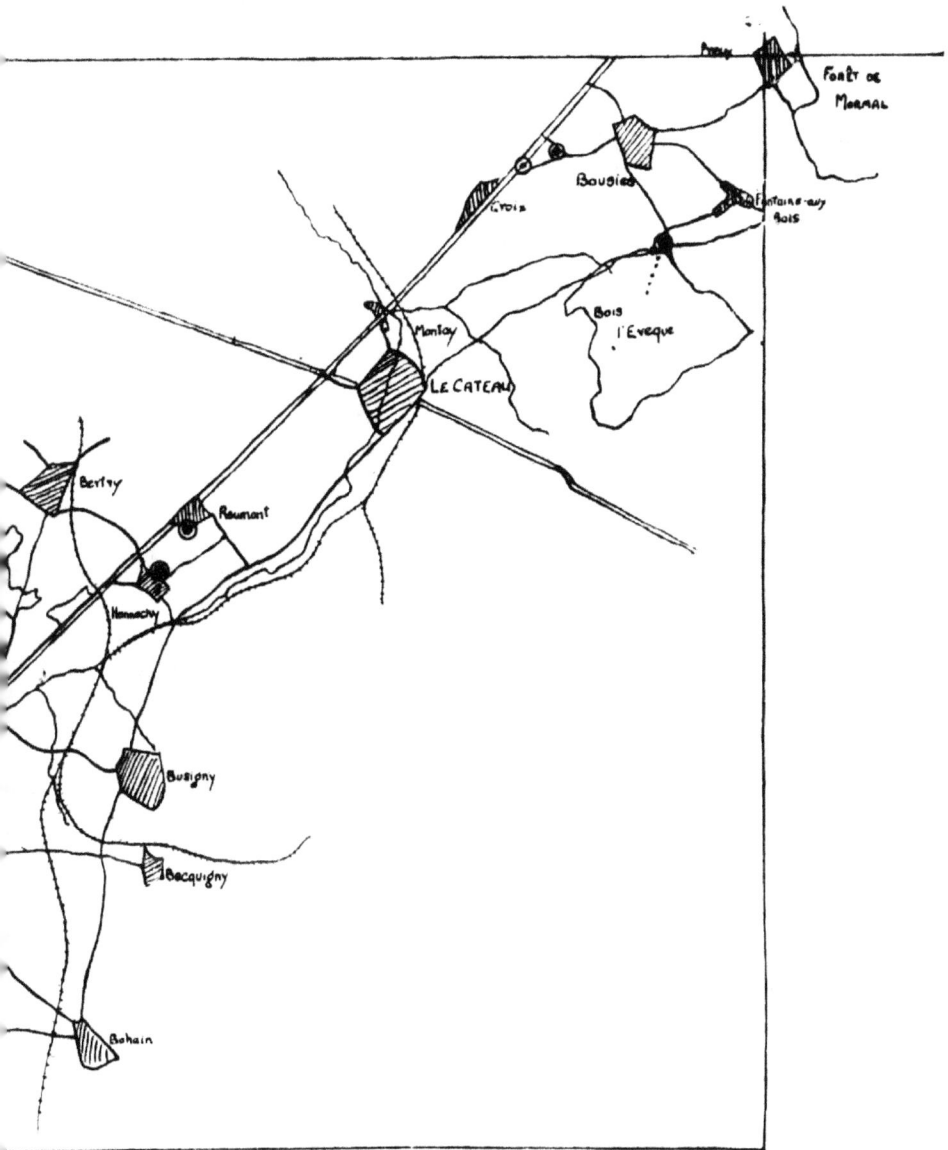

Preux

Forêt de
Mormal

Croix

Bougies

Fontaine-aux
Bois

Bois
l'Eveque

Montay

LE CATEAU

Bertry

Reumont

Honnechy

Busigny

Bacquigny

Bohain

"BRINGING UP THE GUNS"
A Selection Of Artillery titles
From

naval-military-press.com

The ROYAL REGIMENT OF ARTILLERY AT LE CATEAU
Major A. F. Becke, late RFA

An artillery historian's account olf his regiment's performance at Le Catreau, the second battle (after Mons) fought by the BEF in 1914. Based on the author's interviews with officers who were there.

9781843425458

A FIELD ARTILLERY GROUP IN BATTLE
Col W.H.F.Weber

A tactical study of a Field Artillery Group in Retreat, in the Advance and in the Surprise, based on the action of 2nd Brigade RFA (6th Division) in the German 1918 Offensive, in the Allied advance to victory September/October 1918, and the Battle of Cambrai.

9781843426707

HANDBOOK OF ARTILLERY INSTRUMENTS 1914
HMSO 1914

The equipment of the gunner: optical instruments, slide rules, survey equipment.

9781843427063

ILLUSTRATED RECORD OF GERMAN ARMY EQUIPMENT 1939-1945
VOLUME II ARTILLERY

Complete listing of all operational German artillery weapons in the Second World War. Includes the super-heavy railway guns as well as 2cm Flak, and all field guns.

9781843427131

A FEW OBSERVATIONS ON THE MODE OF ATTACK AND EMPLOYMENT OF THE HEAVY ARTILLERY AT CIUDAD RODRIGO AND BADAJOZ IN 1812 AND ST. SEBASTIAN IN 1813

Brevet Lt Col. Sir John May R.H.A.

Veteran artillery officer's analysis of the sieges of Badajoz and Ciudad Roderigo in the Peninsula War, and the reasons for their successful storming.

9781843429425

NOTES ON THE EARLY HISTORY OF THE ROYAL REGIMENT OF ARTILLERY (TO 1757)

The Late Colonel Cleaveland, RA, Edited, with Notes, by Lieut.-Col W. L. Yonge)

Official history of the Royal Regiment of Artillery down to 1757. Packed with a wealth of arcane information and detail.

9781845740412

NINE DAYS
Adventures of a Heavy Artillery Brigade of the Third Army during the German Offensive of March 21-29 1918

Arthur Behrend

A Gunner's experiences of the opening days of Ludendorff's great offensive launched on March 21st 1918. The author was a Brigade adjutant and gives a memorable picture of the attack and its aftermath as seen by the artillery arm.

9781847349811

THE HISTORY OF THE ROYAL AND INDIAN ARTILLERY IN THE MUTINY OF 1857
Col. Julian R. J. Jocelyn
A history of the Royal Artillery's role and the three Indian artillery regiment's part in the Indian Mutiny from Delhi to Lucknow. Appendices list awards, rolls of honour etc.
9781843429678

HISTORY OF THE ROYAL ARTILLERY (CRIMEAN PERIOD)
Col. Julian R. Jocelyn
Detailed history of the Royal Artillery during the Crimea - a war in which guns played a big part. A superbly illustrated, interesting official account.
9781845745547

29TH DIVISIONAL ARTILLERY WAR RECORD AND HONOURS BOOK 1915-1918.
Lt Col R.M.Johnson
This record contains the list of honours awarded to officers and men, with citations; the casualty lists of officers and men killed or wounded; the record of service of officers who served with the divisional artillery between Gallipoli and the armistice, and a brief account of the doings of the divisional artillery from January 1915 to March 1919.
9781843429760

HISTORY of the 33RD DIVISIONAL ARTILLERY in the War 1914-1918
J. Macartney-Filgate, late Major. Foreword General Lord Horne
The 33rd Divisional Artillery served on the Western Front from December 1915 to the armistice. This record gives details of the sectors of the front where batteries were engaged, lists all the other divisions supported by 33rd Divisional Artillery, and lists all casualties, year by year, officers by name other ranks numerically.
9781843429784

ARTILLERY AND TRENCH MORTAR MEMORIES - 32ND DIVISION
Ed R.Whinyates

Personal diaries and memories of officers and men who fought with the 32nd Divisional Artillery, the main feature being the diary of the 32nd Divisional Artillery chaplain from June 1916 to October 1919, which covers some 500 pages and is an outstanding piece of work.

9781843429777

THE HISTORY OF THE 13TH BATTERY, ROYAL FIELD ARTILLERY, FROM 1759 TO 1913
Major H. Marriott Smith

A brief history of a field artillery battery that served in Egypt(1800), at Corunna, in the Crimea and in the Boer War. Battery movements, pay, establishments and sucession of battery OCs.

9781845740498

naval-military-press.com

www.ingramcontent.com/pod-product-compliance
Lightning Source LLC
LaVergne TN
LVHW051159080426
835508LV00021B/2715